INSIGHT GUIDES

LONDON
StepbyStep

WITHDRAWN

APA PUBLICATIONS L
Part of the Langenscheidt Publishing Group

OVERVIEW

An overview of London's geography, customs and culture, plus illuminating background information on food and drink, shopping, entertainment and history.

CITY INTRODUCTION

Fire, plague, population explosions, aerial bombing, economic recessions, urban blight, terrorism… London has taken everything history could throw at it, and this has made it one of the world's most complex and fascinating cities.

Mother Tongue

A recent survey found that more than 300 languages (from Akan to Zulu) are spoken by London's school-children. After English, the most widely spoken are Bengali and Sylheti, Panjabi, Gujarati, and Hindi/Urdu.

Below: parliament and Whitehall.

There must be something special about London to attract more than 27 million overnight visitors each year. And it is not the weather. There are, however, wonderful palaces and cathedrals, theatres and museums, parks and gardens, restaurants serving cuisine from all parts of the world, a vibrant nightlife, and a refreshingly cosmopolitan and open attitude towards diversity in all things, especially its own inhabitants.

POPULATION

Population Growth

The population of London is estimated at over 7.8 million people and there is no sign of any let up in its growth. London is generally considered the most populous city in the European Union (EU). Of course, there are questions over where the boundaries of London's sprawl lie, but it is usually defined as the financial district ('the City') and the 32 boroughs that constitute 'Greater London'.

The population on this territory rose from about 1.1 million in 1801 to peak at over 8.6 million in 1939. It then declined to 6.7 million in 1988, before growing once more to about the same level today as in 1970 (also the level of the 1920s). However, the wider metropolitan area of London continues to spread outwards and is now home to between 12 and 14 million, depending on the definition of that area.

Ethnicity

More than one in three London residents is from a minority ethnic group. Figures from the Office for National Statistics show that, as of 2008, London's foreign-born population is 2.3 million (32 percent), up from 1.6 million in 1997. Of this number, about

39 percent are from the Indian subcontinent and about 35 percent are African or Afro-Caribbean. In addition, there has recently been an influx of hundreds of thousands of workers from the new member countries of the EU, particularly Poland.

Of course, London has been a focus of immigration for centuries, whether as a place of safety (as with the Huguenots fleeing Catholic France, or Eastern European Jews escaping Nazism) or for economic reasons (as with the Irish, Bangladeshis and West Indians).

Wealth Distribution

London ranks as one of the most expensive cities in the world, alongside Tokyo and Moscow. At one end of the scale, London is ranked third in the world in number of billionaire residents. There is also the City of London, renowned for awarding stellar bonuses to its star employees.

At the other end of the scale are the down-and-outs sleeping rough in shop doorways, and newly arrived economic immigrants living in cramped boarding houses. In the past, the East End hosted countless impoverished arrivals from overseas. Many have subsequently moved elsewhere in London as they have gained prosperity. A higher percentage of Indians and Pakistanis, for example, now own their own homes in the capital than white people.

Above from far left: Millennium Bridge and St Paul's; Coldstream Guard at the Changing the Guard ceremony outside Buckingham Palace; the London Eye; taxi at night.

Sport in London
Even if your visit to London does not coincide with the 2012 Olympics, there is still plenty on offer: world-class football at Arsenal and Chelsea; cricket at Lord's and the Oval; tennis at Wimbledon; horse racing a short train ride away at Ascot; rugby at Twickenham; and boxing at Bethnal Green's York Hall.

London Cabbies

About 20,000 drivers work in London, half of them as owner-drivers. The others either hire vehicles from big fleets or work night shifts in someone else's cab. Would-be drivers must register with the Public Carriage Office and then spend up to four years learning London in minute detail – known as 'the Knowledge'. They achieve this by travelling the streets of the metropolis on a moped, whatever the weather, working out a multitude of routes from a clipboard mounted on the handlebars. So even if the supposedly garrulous cabbies do not always know what they are talking about, they do know where they are going. The classic cab itself – or Hackney Carriage, as it is officially known – is the FX4, launched in 1959, and still going strong in its updated incarnation (with full wheelchair access). The traditional manner for hailing a cab is to raise your arm and shout, 'Taxi!' The cab may not always stop though: Prince Philip and the comedian Stephen Fry are known to maintain their own black cabs, so that they can travel around the city in anonymity.

Above: black cab; blue plaque.

Frost Fairs

Between 1400 and 1900 there were 23 winters in which the river Thames froze over at London. When the ice was thick enough and lasted long enough, festivals were held on the river, featuring everything from skating to bull-baiting to horse races, and even, at the last frost fair, in 1814, an elephant, led across below Blackfriars Bridge. The river has not frozen over since then: the climate has grown milder, old London Bridge (which had slowed up the river flow) was demolished in 1831, and the river has been embanked, making it deeper and less liable to freezing.

THE CLIMATE

London has a mild climate. Snow (other than a light dusting) and temperatures below freezing are fairly unusual, with January temperatures averaging 4°C (39°F). In the summer months, temperatures average 17°C (63°F), but can rise much higher, causing the city to become stiflingly hot (air conditioning is not universal). Heat stored by the city's buildings creates a microclimate with temperatures up to 5 °C (9 °F) warmer in the city than in the surrounding areas. Even so, summer temperatures rarely rise much above 33 °C (91.4 °F), and the highest temperature ever recorded in London was 38.1 °C (100.6 °F), measured at Kew Gardens during the European heat wave of 2003.

Day to day fluctuations can be significant, though, and surprise showers catch people unprepared all year round. This enables people to engage in a favourite topic of conversation and to tut-tut over inclement spells. Whatever the season, visitors should come prepared with wet-weather clothes (a mackintosh or other waterproof coat) and other useful apparatus (umbrella, headscarf, hat, etc).

LONDON GEOGRAPHY

The Political Map

When people talk about London, they are usually referring to the area covered by Greater London. This administrative organisation was imposed on the city in 1965. It comprises the City of

London and 32 London boroughs.

Originally, there were two cities here: the City of Westminster (centred on the Houses of Parliament and Westminster Abbey) and the City of London (often referred to simply as 'the City', and covering what is now the financial district – the historic square mile between St Paul's Cathedral and the Tower of London). Westminster is now a borough just like any other, governed by a borough council. The City of London, on the other hand, has its own unique institutions of local government dating back to the 12th century: the Corporation of London, headed by the Lord Mayor.

Presiding over Greater London at the top level is the Greater London Authority (GLA) with, at its head, a directly elected mayor (not to be confused with the Lord Mayor of the City of London). The Mayor and the GLA are responsible for the Metropolitan Police Authority, the London Fire and Emergency Planning Authority, the London Development Agency and Transport for London. Services such as refuse disposal, housing grants and parking control are run at local level by the boroughs.

North–South, East–West

Whatever the political subdivisions of London, the physical and social ones are often more significant. Not least of these is the River Thames, dividing the city into north and south. London north of the river has historically been the location of government and commerce. The south, apart from the river

banks themselves, was less developed until the 19th century, when it became a vast residential suburb. South London is still much less of a destination for a day out than north London, and cab drivers, notoriously, sometimes refuse to take passengers south of the river.

West London, especially Mayfair, Kensington and Chelsea, is the posh end of town. It is now particularly popular with wealthy foreign residents, attracted by the relative security of the area, the investment potential of owning one of its smart properties, and Britain's lenient tax regime. East London, on the other hand, has historically harboured some of the poorest communities in the city, with the indigenous working classes, close by London's docks, living alongside newly arrived immigrants. Parts of it are now far more vibrant than west London, popular with artists and a younger, more outward-looking generation.

HEAVEN AND HELL

The 18th-century man of letters, Samuel Johnson, famously declared, 'When a man is tired of London, he is tired of life; for there is in London all that life can afford.' This is still the case today: London offers some the chance to accumulate great wealth, others to be at the centre of cultural ferment, and many others the opportunity simply to be themselves in a tolerant and civilised environment (no matter what their creed or colour, sexual orientation or chosen lifestyle). However, at times, London has

seemed less than idyllic. In 1819, the poet Shelley wrote, 'Hell is a city much like London/A populous and smoky city.' Indeed, at one time, the streets in the old City were so dark and narrow that shopkeepers had to erect mirrors outside their windows to reflect light into the shops. And pollution and congestion are still problems today, warranting the city's widely used nickname, 'The Big Smoke'.

The last 25 years, though, have seen something of a renaissance for the city, with the regeneration of neglected areas, a vibrant art and music scene, fuller employment, and even some improvements in public transport. This atmosphere of optimism and confidence reached its apogee in the late 90s, when London was the centre of what the media referred to as 'Cool Britannia', and was a magnet for many an aspiring mover and shaker.

Above from far left: bird's-eye view of the Thames; hip local; deckchairs in Hyde Park; St Pancras.

Camden

As much a part of the 'Britpop' music scene as anywhere in London, Camden (north of Euston Station) is the location of numerous clubs, bars and other venues where many famous bands played their first gigs. Try Barfly, the Jazz Café, the Dublin Castle, or the Bull and Gate. There is also a huge market around Camden Lock where you can buy the clothes to perfect that retro look.

Below: tea at the Ritz.

FOOD AND DRINK

London's cuisine was once reputed to offer little more than overcooked stodge. Not so now: as well as impressive renditions of just about every other country's cuisine, you can appreciate the finest of Britain's own food heritage.

Above: spoon, fork and napkin; decorative flowers; and coffee – all at Vinoteca *(see p.61)*.

Top from left: bastion of traditional British dining, Simpson's in the Strand; Terence Conran's Bibendum, in the former Michelin tyre headquarters, Fulham Road; bottles of olive oil; classic British fish and chips.

Opposite: bookish Asia de Cuba.

The last few decades have seen a remarkable transformation in London's restaurant scene, bringing it into the international league. Londoners' taste for innovative cooking of the best produce has made the city the envy of foreign capitals more traditionally regarded as gastronomically blessed. At one time, however, things were very different, and British food was the butt of many jokes, especially from the French. Jacques Chirac is quoted as saying that 'you can't trust people who cook as badly as that'. Nowadays, a good pork chop from St John or Scottish lobster at Gordon Ramsay would have him eating his words.

BRITISH CUISINE

As well as a great enthusiasm for foreign styles of cooking, the blossoming of London's restaurant scene is closely related to the re-evaluation of Britain's indigenous cuisine. A new generation of energetic head chefs has proved emphatically that British food is much more than meat and two veg, a stodgy pie full of gravy or a buttie stuffed with soggy chips. Now you can find Cromer crab, Cornish sprats, Gressingham duck, juicy Herdwick lamb, Galloway beef, and traditional desserts such as Eccles cakes with Lancashire cheese or bread-and-butter pudding. This newfound culinary zeal has filtered down to the local pub, where potted shrimps, shepherd's pie, Lancashire hotpot and bangers and mash are cooked with care and served with pride.

PLACES TO EAT

High-End Restaurants

As well as long-established stalwarts such as Le Gavroche, in recent years London has nurtured numerous other Michelin-star contenders. Gordon Ramsay, Marcus Wareing, Tom Aikens, and Angela Hartnett among others have all raised expectations of what restaurants should be offering.

The food at many top restaurants is based on French cooking techniques. Even the so-called 'modern British' style is founded on a combination of high-quality British ingredients with French methods of preparation. For interesting alternatives try the River Café, with its unpretentious modern Italian cooking, or Benares for innovative Indian dishes.

It is easily argued that many restaurants in London give too much emphasis to design and image and not enough to the food itself. At Sketch or China Tang for example, some feel that if the food is fairly good, it is so

as not to distract from the interior decoration. A step further are the likes of The Ivy or Cipriani, where it is the other diners, some of them celebrities, that are the focus of attention.

Many of the restaurants mentioned above require booking weeks, perhaps months, in advance. Beware also, if they take your credit card details when you book, you may be charged anyway if you do not then show up.

Pubs

If all this business of booking weeks ahead, hefty bills and embarrassing formality is more than you can take, do not fret; all is not lost. Many of the best eating experiences in London are quite inexpensive, relaxed affairs.

A major component of British social history is the public house, which in recent years has been re-evaluated. There is a lot to be said for a pie and a pint. For pub food is a distinctive cuisine in itself (and that does not mean ploughman's lunch with a limp lettuce leaf and a wedge of cheese). Think of steak-and-kidney pudding, meat loaf, Lancashire hotpot, shepherd's pie, sausage and mash and the traditional Sunday roast. If well executed, these dishes can be delicious.

Lots of traditional pubs have now been converted into 'gastro-pubs', many of them sensitively, some crassly. The cliché is of a pub desecrated: its centuries-old patina stripped away, floorboards sanded down, walls painted white, shabby-chic furniture brought in and a blackboard advertising faux-Mediterranean dishes.

However, when it is done well, the gastro-pub can be very good. Try The Anchor and Hope in Southwark, or The Coach and Horses on the edge of the City, or The Cow on Westbourne Park Road near Notting Hill.

Ethnic Restaurants

Another mainstay of London's culinary heritage is the huge variety of ethnic restaurants, especially Indian, Chinese, Japanese, Vietnamese and Thai. According to city authorities, 53 major country styles are represented among the 6,000 licensed restaurants. Visit Kingsland Road in the East End for Vietnamese and Turkish, Whitechapel or Tooting (south London) for Indian, and Stockwell (also south of the river) for Portuguese establishments.

Fish and Chips

Whereas in the 1930s there were more than 30,000 fish and chip shops in Britain, today there are only 8,600. The future of those remaining is threatened by dwindling fish stocks and fast-food corporations. In the past, cod was preferred in the south of Britain and haddock in the north. It is skate, however, which is the real test of a fryer's mettle: if cooked just right, it is soft and light, but if only 90 percent cooked, it is a glutinous, bony mess.

Beer Flood
In 1814, at a brewery on Tottenham Court Road, a huge vat containing over 135,000 gallons (511,000 litres) of beer ruptured, causing other vats in the same building to do the same, in a domino effect. More than 323,000 gallons (1,223,000 litres) of beer gushed into the streets. The tsunami of beer destroyed two homes and knocked down the wall of the Tavistock Arms pub, trapping the barmaid under the rubble. In all, nine people were killed: eight due to drowning, one from alcohol poisoning. The brewery was eventually taken to court over the accident, but the judge and jury ruled the disaster to be an 'Act of God'.

Greasy Spoons, Pie and Mash and Fish and Chips

Often overlooked is London's fast-disappearing old-fashioned, working-class grub. Even 15 years ago there was always a haven close at hand offering a plate of piping hot food at everyday prices. Now, the greasy spoon caffs, fish and chip, and pie and mash shops are being usurped by coffee bars and fast-food corporations that can pay grasping landlords' higher rents.

'Greasy spoon' cafés serve all-day breakfasts: eggs, bacon, chips and beans, sometimes with manly extras such as black pudding or bubble and squeak. Also, strong tea and white bread and butter. Check out www.classiccafes. co.uk for an anthology of the best greasy spoon caffs still open.

Pie and mash shops serve meat pies or eels (jellied or stewed) with liquor (an odd sort of glop based on parsley sauce) and mashed potato. The premises themselves have wonderful tiled interiors, marble-topped tables and wooden benches. Good examples are Manze's on Tower Bridge Road and F. Cooke on Broadway Market in the East End.

Lastly come the fish and chip shops, with their fat stubby fried potatoes, quite impossible to replicate in a conventional kitchen, and fish in batter, double fried. Try Fryer's Delight on Theobald's Road *(see p.119)* and Rock & Sole Plaice in Covent Garden *(see p.37)*.

Chains

London has ever more chain restaurants, more indeed than most other European cities. Some are reasonably good (Carluccio's or Leon for example), others are hugely disappointing, with food microwaved from frozen, and staff as apathetic as you might expect on the minimum wage. Remarkably, it is sometimes the affluent areas (Hampstead, for example) that are the most intensive breeding ground for chains and have little else to offer besides.

DRINKS

Beer

Traditionally, beer was to Britain what wine was to France. It comes in various forms, from lager (now the most popular form in Britain) to ale (brewed using only top-fermenting yeasts; sweeter and fuller bodied) to stout (creamy, almost coffee-like beer made from roasted malts or roast barley), of which the most famous brand is probably Guinness.

Pubs generally serve beer either 'draught' or from the cask. In the case of the former, a keg is pressurised with carbon-dioxide gas, which drives the beer to the dispensing tap. For the latter, beer is pulled from the cask via a beer line with a hand pump at the bar. This method is generally used for what is often termed 'real ale': unfiltered and unpasteurised beer, which, unlike industrially produced lagers, requires careful storage at the correct temperature.

Wine

The popularity of wine-drinking in Britain has increased dramatically in the last few decades. In the unen-

lightened days, many pubs served only Liebfraumilch or Lambrusco, but nowadays you can expect a more grown-up selection, and New World wines are at least as widely offered by pubs as European wines. The growing popularity of wine in Britain has even encouraged some growers to start producing English varieties. Try the restaurant, Roast *(see p.67)*, upstairs at Borough Market, for a good-quality selection of English wines.

Cider

A longer-established English tipple is cider, produced in southwest England since before the Romans arrived. Made from the fermented juice of apples, it is also known as 'scrumpy' (windfalls are 'scrumps'). The pear equivalent is called 'perry'. Unfortunately, many pubs only offer mass-produced cider made from apple concentrate. For the real thing, try The Blackfriar *(see p.55)*, The Harp on Chandos Place, tucked just behind St-Martin-in-the-Fields *(see walk 1)*, or Chimes restaurant on Churton Street in Pimlico.

Whisky

Another speciality is whisky, produced in Scotland and Ireland. This is available as 'single malt' (malt whisky from a single distillery), as well as 'blended' – cheaper whiskies are normally made from a mixture of malt and grain whiskies from many distilleries. Most pubs in central London will offer a small selection of both, though aficionados may consider joining the Whisky Society, which has its mem-

bers' rooms above the Bleeding Heart Restaurant in Hatton Garden, Clerkenwell (Bleeding Heart Yard; tel: 020-7831 4447; www.smws.co.uk).

Last Orders

Most pubs ring a bell for 'last orders' at 11pm and then expect you to drink up and depart by 11.30pm. In 2003 new legislation was introduced allowing pub landlords to apply for extended opening hours, up to 24 hours a day, seven days a week. In practice (although many now stay open throughout the afternoon), only a small minority of pubs made such an application. However, this has not stopped renewed concern about Britain's supposed 'binge-drinking' culture.

Above from far left: afternoon tea at Brown's Hotel; profiteroles *(left)* and grilled fish *(right)*, at St John Bread and Wine *(see p.89)*; The Laughing Gravy.

Curry
A recent foreign secretary, Robin Cook, claimed chicken tikka masala was 'Britain's true national dish'. Indeed, Britain's Indian and Pakistani restaurants employ more people than the coal, steel and ship-building industries combined.

Food Markets

Perhaps the best of London's food markets for the visitor is Borough Market near London Bridge (Thur 11am–5pm, Fri noon–6pm, Sat 9am–4pm). It offers some of the country's best produce in an historic setting. For other farmers' markets, see www.lfm.org.uk. London's main wholesale markets are Smithfields for meat (Mon–Fri 4–10am), Billingsgate for fish (now in Docklands; offers some guided tours; Tue–Sat 5–8.30am) and Spitalfields for fruit and vegetables (now in Leyton; Mon–Fri midnight–1pm, Sat until 11am).

SHOPPING

Napoleon called England a nation of shopkeepers. Perhaps he had a point.
Whether you are in the market for a grand piano or a custom-made brassiere,
a pet parrot or a snuff box, there will be somewhere in London you can buy it.

Above: ready to
wear; jeans at Top-
shop, the world's
largest fashion store;
Jeremy Fisher at Peter
Rabbit & Friends,
Covent Garden.

Opening Hours
Most shops open from
9 or 10am until 6 or
6.30pm, with no break
for lunch. West End
shops usually open
late on Thursday, until
around 7 or 8pm.
Many shops open
on Sundays, although
with shorter hours.

With more than 30,000 shops, and
everything available, from Old Masters
to vintage film posters, Savile Row suits
to punk-rock T-shirts, London is an
easy place to spend your cash. And just
to make it even easier, unlike in many
other European capitals, Sundays and
summer holidays are not sacred: this
is a year-round shopper's destination.

SHOPPING AREAS

For those on a retail mission, the sheer
size of the city means you have to be
selective. However, London's shopping
geography is relatively easy to navigate
and can be loosely divided into shopping districts, each offering a distinctive experience. Indeed, in some
cases there are whole streets devoted to
one theme: Savile Row and Jermyn
Street for gentlemen's outfitters, Hatton Garden for jewellery, Carnaby
Street for branded street fashion.

The best means for getting from area
to area is usually the tube, though for the
journey home, those laiden with heavy
bags may favour a taxi. The bus network
has good coverage, but is slower and less
easy to navigate. And of course, there
is always a lot to be said for walking: distances between some streets – Oxford
Street and Piccadilly, Regent Street and
Bond Street – are short enough to walk.

Designer Districts

For those wanting the best of European
and international designer fashions,
Knightsbridge, home to the higher-end
department stores Harrods and Harvey
Nichols, has perhaps the highest con-
centration of such shops. Haute couture
names from Armani to Yves Saint
Laurent sit next to established British
designers Katharine Hamnett, Anya
Hindmarch and Bruce Oldfield, to
name a few. Also out west are the King's
Road and Fulham Road in Chelsea,
with couturiers such as Anne Fontaine
and Amanda Wakeley sandwiched
between smart interior design stores.

Bond Street, in Mayfair, also offers a
vast choice of designer labels as well as
the world's biggest names in jewellery,
and some of London's top dealers in Old
Masters and antique furniture. Cork
Street, the next road along, is lined with
dealers in modern art, while a little further east still is Savile Row.

Around Piccadilly

Around the Piccadilly area are some of
London's oldest shops, many of which
hold royal warrants to supply the
Queen and her family with goods. On
Piccadilly itself are up-market grocer
Fortnum & Mason and Hatchards the
booksellers. Parallel with Piccadilly is
Jermyn Street, which specialises in

shirts, though it is also the place for the debonair to find a silk dressing gown or a pair of monogrammed carpet slippers. On St James's, just nearby, is Lock's the hatters, and Lobb's the bootmakers. Then there is Regent Street, the world's first purpose-built shopping street, running north from Piccadilly Circus, and home to Britain's largest toy shop, Hamleys, as well as Liberty, the Arts and Crafts shopping institution.

Chains and Department Stores

High-street chains and department stores characterise Oxford Street, the capital's main shopping thoroughfare. Selfridges and John Lewis, near Bond Street tube, are perhaps the only destination shops here. Near Oxford Circus, running south, is Carnaby Street *(see left)*. Finally, at the eastern end of Oxford Street is Tottenham Court Road, dominated by electronics and hi-fi shops, as well as home furnishings stores, including Habitat and Heal's.

Soho and Covent Garden

Although Soho has never quite lost its seedy atmosphere, in between the sex shops there are some fine delicatessens, as well as stores selling hip urban wear. Bookworms should head for nearby Charing Cross Road (and Cecil Court, too), with its second-hand bookshops and major branches of large book chains.

Covent Garden offers high-street and urban fashion as well as specialist emporia dedicated to teapots or kites or cheese or wooden toys.

MARKETS

London has markets for antiques, crafts, clothes and, of course, food *(see p.17)*. For antiques enthusiasts, Portobello Road is the obvious choice, with the main market held on Saturdays. An alternative is Alfies Antique Market (Tue–Sat 10am–6pm) on Church Street near Marylebone. For a more up-market affair, try the shops on Kensington Church Street, where more than 80 dealers display their finds.

For clothes and crafts, in the East End there are weekend markets at Spitalfields and Brick Lane, as well as the weekday rag trade in Petticoat Lane (also Sunday morning). Then there is Portobello Road (retro) and Camden Lock (retro, clubwear, goth and punk). At Greenwich market (Thur–Sun) the emphasis is on crafts and deli foods.

Above from far left: multicoloured paper at Papyrus; shoes in up-market Mayfair; dummies at Harrods; flowers on sale in South Kensington.

The Sales
There are two main sales periods across the UK – January, and July and August. Prices may be slashed by up to 50 percent and more, especially on large items or last season's fashions.

Below: Harrods Art-Nouveau food hall.

ENTERTAINMENT

Whether you prefer to get engrossed in the latest cinematic release, listen to a world-class rendition of Mahler, enjoy classic drama, a lively musical, or the latest R&B, London can offer the appropriate venue.

An international city such as London is large and densely populated enough to support a bewildering variety of entertainment venues. It shows particular strength in theatre and music venues, though in film and dance it is certainly no slouch either. Meanwhile, the young and young at heart enjoy the capital's reputation as one of the great international clubbing centres, with every kind of music and a vibrant gay scene. But not all nightlife is dance-till-dawn. Older visitors can enjoy pubs, bars and jazz clubs.

Below: crest of the Royal Opera House; street piano for the public in Leicester Square, part of a temporary project; Odeon is a large cinema chain.

THEATRE

London's Theatreland is in the West End – in particular around Piccadilly, Shaftesbury Avenue, Charing Cross Road, The Strand and Covent Garden. Here, the tradition is as much about the theatres themselves as the quality of the drama. This is where velvet-and-gilt Victorian playhouses were designed so that most of the audience would peer down over the stage, where 'the gods' (the seats high at the back) bring on vertigo, and where it is difficult to escape the concern that, had the buildings been conceived today, fire regulations would have ensured that they never left the architects' drawing boards.

Nevertheless, the West End is still a theatrical magnet, because this is where the money is. Catering for audiences by the coach-load, impresarios look to musical spectacles, revivals, and to plays that will please the widest range of tastes. As a result, such middle-of-the-road creative types as composer Andrew Lloyd Webber and producer Cameron Mackintosh have become both famous and very rich.

Drama Old and New

Many theatre lovers claim that the mania for musicals squeezes out new drama productions. Yet a glance through the theatre listings doesn't entirely bear out this claim. Classics are interpreted anew at the Donmar Warehouse in Covent Garden and at the National Theatre and Old and Young Vic just south of the river; and Shakespeare's Globe has been a triumph of culture over commercialism. Meanwhile, new writing is still put on at the Royal Court, and experimental work and alternative comedy are mounted at numerous fringe theatres.

MUSIC

London has an active and varied music scene, with plenty to cater to every musical taste. For the latest

music, the clubs and bars of Camden in North London are good hunting grounds for up-and-coming bands. Many famous artists played their first gigs at Barfly, for example, and young hopefuls continue to do so today. If, on the other hand, jazz is more your style, then Ronnie Scott's in Soho is the best-known venue, showcasing top international artists.

Classical music enthusiasts will find numerous professional orchestras in the capital. Perhaps the best at the moment is the London Symphony Orchestra, which usually performs at the Barbican. Several of the other orchestras – including the Philharmonia – are based at the Royal Festival Hall on the South Bank. Then in the summer, there is the BBC-sponsored Proms festival of around 100 concerts at the Royal Albert Hall in South Kensington. Many of the world's greatest orchestras and soloists feature in the line ups, while the famous Last Night is performed by the redoubtable BBC Symphony Orchestra.

For opera enthusiasts, there are the Royal Opera and English National Opera companies. The Royal Opera House in Covent Garden, home to the Royal Opera, is a magnificent theatre presenting lavish performances in the original language. Tickets are expensive, unless you are prepared to stand or accept a distant view. English National Opera's home is the London Coliseum on St Martin's Lane. Ticket prices are lower than at Covent Garden and can sometimes be bought on the night of a performance.

FILM

If you want to see the latest Hollywood blockbusters in Central London, the place to go is Leicester Square *(see p. 41)*, where the big multiplex cinemas are clustered. Ticket prices are high, but audiences benefit from the high-quality projection and sound systems. If art-house cinema is more your style, just a short walk north, in Soho, is the main branch of the Curzon cinema chain (www.curzoncinemas.com), which shows all the latest releases.

Meanwhile, south of the river at the Southbank Centre is the British Film Institute, a government-subsidised organisation that screens classic and cult films of the past, and organises film festivals and themed seasons. The BFI also runs the Imax cinema near Waterloo Station, which shows blockbuster, animated, and 3-D films on its vast screen.

NIGHTLIFE

London has several nightlife scenes. Hoxton and Shoreditch in the East End are home to the hippest nightspots, where DJ bars and 'pop-up' nightclubs are congregated. For large-scale clubs featuring the latest popular music, Leicester Square and Covent Garden are the main destinations. Camden *(see left)* is a good option for live-music venues. The gay clubbing scene is concentrated in Vauxhall, south of the river, while Soho's Old Compton and Brewer streets accommodate many gay pubs and cabaret venues.

Above from far left: the National Theatre; the historic auditorium at the Royal Opera House.

Dance

For ballet, London's major venues are the Royal Opera House and the London Coliseum, home to the Royal Ballet and English National Ballet respectively. For contemporary dance, the main venue is Sadler's Wells, in Islington, to the north of the City. Its state-of-the-art performance spaces are used for innovative programmes featuring many top artists. Sadler's Wells also operates from a West End venue – the Peacock Theatre on Portugal Street, just north of Aldwych.

HISTORY: KEY DATES

From humble beginnings, through sacking, fire, pestilence and war, and with renowned pomp and circumstance, London has grown to become one of the world's most culturally vibrant, cosmopolitan and ethnically diverse capitals.

EARLY PERIOD

AD 43	Emperor Claudius establishes the trade port of Londinium and builds a bridge over the River Thames.
61	Boudicca sacks the city but is defeated, and London is rebuilt.
c.200	City wall built. London is made the capital of Britannia Superior.
410	Romans withdraw to defend Rome. London falls into decline.
604	The first St Paul's Cathedral is founded by King Ethelbert.
c.750	The monastery of St Peter is founded on Thorney Island; it later becomes Westminster Abbey.
884	London becomes the capital under Alfred the Great.
1042	Edward the Confessor moves his court to Westminster.

AFTER THE CONQUEST

1066	William I, Duke of Normandy, conquers Britain.
1078	Tower of London's White Tower is built.
1191	London elects its first mayor, Henry Fitzailwin.
1348–9	Black Death wipes out about 50 percent of London's population.
1534	Henry VIII declares himself head of the Church of England.
1558–1603	London is the capital of a mighty kingdom under Elizabeth I.
1599	The Globe theatre opens at Bankside.
1605	Guy Fawkes attempts to blow up James I and Parliament.
1642–9	Civil war between Cavalier Royalists and republican Roundheads. Royalists are defeated; Charles I is executed.
1660	The monarchy is restored under Charles II.
1664–6	Plague hits London again, killing around 110,000 citizens.
1666	Great Fire of London destroys 80 percent of London's buildings.

Above: Henry Fitzailwin, the first mayor of London; detail of The Globe from Visscher's map of London; Guy Fawkes and his fellow conspirators plot to blow up parliament and King James I.

AFTER THE FIRE

1675	Sir Christopher Wren begins to rebuild St Paul's Cathedral.
1764	The Literary Club is established by Samuel Johnson, compiler of the first English dictionary.

1783	Last execution held at Tyburn (Marble Arch).
1803–15	Napoleonic Wars.
1811–20	Era of Prince Regent, later George IV; Regency style.
1824	Establishment of the National Gallery.
1834	Building starts on the Gothic-style Houses of Parliament that are still standing today, after the old Palace of Westminster burns down.

Above: historic depiction of the Thames, painted c.1822, by Robert Havell Jr.

THE AGE OF EMPIRE

1837–1901	Queen Victoria's reign, characterised by Empire building and the Industrial Revolution.
1849	Tea merchant Henry Charles Harrod opens a shop in Knightsbridge.
1851	The hugely successful Great Exhibition is held in architect Joseph Paxton's Crystal Palace in Hyde Park.
1859	'Big Ben' bell is hung in the tower of the Palace of Westminster.
1863	London Underground opens its first line, the Metropolitan line.
1888	The serial murderer dubbed Jack the Ripper strikes in Whitechapel.

20TH CENTURY

1914–18	World War I. Zeppelins bomb London.
1922	British Broadcasting Company transmits its first radio programmes.
1939–45	World War II. London is heavily bombed, killing 29,000 people and damaging 80 percent and destroying a third of buildings in the City.
1951	Festival of Britain. Southbank Centre built adjacent to Waterloo.
1960s	London christened the capital of hip for fashion, music and the arts.
1980s	Margaret Thatcher years. Several IRA bombs hit London.
1986	The Greater London Council is abolished by Thatcher.
1996	The new Shakespeare's Globe opens on Bankside.
1997	New Labour elected under Tony Blair. 'Cool Britannia' period.

21ST CENTURY

2000	Dome, London Eye, Tate Modern and Jubilee Line extension open to celebrate the millennium. Ken Livingstone elected mayor.
2001	Greater London Authority is re-established under Mayor Livingstone.
2005	Terrorist bomb attacks on 7 July kill 52 and injure about 700.
2008	Boris Johnson elected mayor.
2010	David Cameron succeeds Gordon Brown as prime minister.
2012	London celebrates the Queen's Diamond Jubilee in June, and hosts the Olympic Games in late July and early August.

Great Exhibition
In 1851 Queen Victoria (1837–1901) opened the Great Exhibition of the Works of all Nations in Hyde Park. Its magnificent glass building, dubbed the 'Crystal Palace', displayed Britain's skills and achievements to the entire world and attracted some 6 million visitors. With the profits of £186,000, Prince Albert (1819–61), Queen Victoria's German-born husband, realised his great ambition: to create temples to the arts and sciences, which blossomed in Kensington's gardens – nicknamed 'Albertopolis'. What was later named the Victoria and Albert Museum opened in 1857, followed by the Royal Albert Hall in 1871, the Albert Memorial in 1872 and the Natural History Museum in 1881.

 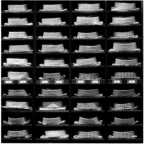 

COVENT

Royal
Academy
of Arts

WALKS AND TOURS

THE BIG SIGHTS

In a changing world it's reassuring that Nelson is still on his column in Trafalgar Square, the prime minister's at No. 10 Downing Street, Big Ben is chiming at the Houses of Parliament and the Queen is at Buckingham Palace.

Above: Nelson's statue dominates Trafalgar Square.

Christmas Tree
Every Christmas since 1947, the Norwegian government has presented a Norway Spruce to the people of London in gratitude for Britain's support during World War II. In the autumn, the Lord Mayor of Westminster visits Oslo to participate in the felling of the tree.

DISTANCE 3 miles (5km)
TIME A full day
START Trafalgar Square
END Buckingham Palace
POINTS TO NOTE

Changing the Guard in Whitehall is at 11am and at Buckingham Palace at 11.30am. A shorter version of this route could start at Trafalgar Square and then skip straight to the Mall section. In summer, last admission to Buckingham Palace is at 4.15pm.

This is the route to do if you are new to London or if you want to revisit the capital's major royal and political sights. Trafalgar Square, where this route begins, is very close to Charing Cross Station and Villiers Street, where we recommend a quick sharpener first at **Gordon's**, see ①①.

TRAFALGAR SQUARE

Trafalgar Square ❶ is plumb in the centre of London, as attested to by the plaque on the traffic island in the south

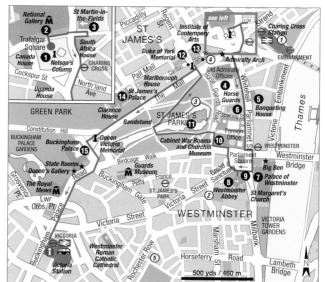

of the square. It was conceived by the Prince Regent in 1820, was designed in its current form by Sir Charles Barry in 1838, and assumed its current name in 1841 in commemoration of Nelson's victory over Napoleon's navy at the Battle of Trafalgar in 1805.

Nelson's Column

At the centre of the square is **Nelson's Column**, a 151ft (46m) granite pillar topped by an 18ft (5.5m) statue of Admiral Lord Nelson. Battle-scarred, with only one arm (though without a patch on his blind eye), he gazes south, surveying the fleet of miniature ships atop the flag poles lining the Mall. Completed in 1843, the column was designed by William Railton, the statue by E.H. Baily. The four iconic lions at the base were added in 1867 by Edwin Landseer, cast from the metal of the cannons of the defeated French fleet.

Flanking the column are two fountains: the originals were replaced in 1939 with larger ones, by Edwin Lutyens, allegedly to limit the space for political demonstrations. In the corners of the square are plinths, with statues of General Charles Napier, Major General Sir Henry Havelock and George IV (astride a horse without a saddle, boots or stirrups); the fourth plinth, originally left empty, is used to display contemporary artworks *(see right)*.

Bordering the Square

Around the square, Canada House, South Africa House and Uganda House are memories of distant Empire days. On the north side of the square is the **National Gallery** ❷ *(covered in detail in walk 2)*, which displays pre-20th-century art. On the lawn in front is a statue of James II by Grinling Gibbons. Hand on hip, he is inexplicably dressed as an ancient Roman. Further along is a diminutive statue of George Washington, a gift from the state of Virginia. He stands on soil imported from the US, honouring his declaration that he would never again set foot on British soil.

St Martin-in-the-Fields

On the east side of the square is **St Martin-in-the-Fields** ❸ (tel: 020-7766 1100; www.stmartin-in-the-fields.org; Mon–Sat 8.30am–6pm, Sun 3.30–5.30pm; free). A church has stood here since the 13th century, when this area was fields between the City of Westminster and the City of London.

The present church was completed in 1726 to designs by James Gibbs. His amalgam of classical and Baroque styles subsequently became the model for many churches in the US. The church was largely paid for by George III, and it remains Buckingham

Above from far left: Changing the Guard at Buckingham Palace; the National Gallery, on Trafalgar Square; one of the fountains in Trafalgar Square; wreath in Whitehall, commemorating World War II.

The Fourth Plinth Trafalgar Square's fourth plinth was left empty after plans in 1841 to erect an equestrian statue collapsed through lack of funds. Recent suggestions for a suitable occupant included Nelson Mandela, Princess Diana and David Beckham. Now, works of art are commissioned to take their turn, each for 18 months. See www.london.gov.uk/fourthplinth for details of the latest exhibit.

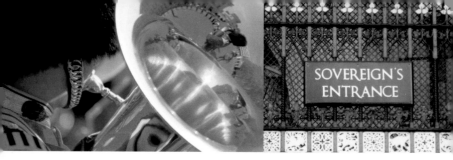

SOVEREIGN'S
ENTRANCE

Above from left:
Scots Guard; royal
entrance at parliament.

Charles I Statue
Facing down Whitehall
from Trafalgar Square
is Hubert le Sueur's
statue of Charles I.
England's first
equestrian bronze,
it was cast in 1633,
then sold for scrap
during the Civil War
and only recovered
and set on its plinth
when the throne was
restored with the reign
of Charles II (1660–85).

WOMEN

War Monuments
In the middle of the
street outside the
Foreign Office stands
the Cenotaph, built by
Edwin Lutyens to
remember those who
died in World War I.
Nearby is a memorial
to the women of
World War II,
depicting sets of
women's work
clothes, hung up at
the end of the war.

Palace's parish church; the box to the left of the gallery is reserved for the royal family.

The church is a venue for concerts of classical music. It also has a Brass Rubbing Centre and a good café. The churchyard outside is the burial site of Charles II's mistress Nell Gwynn, William Hogarth and Joshua Reynolds.

WHITEHALL

Leave Trafalgar Square and head south down Whitehall, named after Henry VIII's palace, which burnt down in 1698. Most of the monumental buildings on this street are government departments, beginning with former Admiralty buildings on your right and the Ministry of Defence on your left.

Horse Guards

On the right, through an arch, is **Horse Guards ❹**, where the Household Cavalry, the Queen's bodyguard on state occasions, mounts the daily Changing the Guard ceremony (www.changing-the-guard.com; Mon–Sat 11am, Sun 10am; free). Cameras click, horses nod, commands are shouted, then the troop returns to barracks.

Banqueting House

On the opposite side of Whitehall from Horse Guards is the **Banqueting House ❺** (tel: 020-7930 4179; www.hrp.org.uk; Mon–Sat 10am–5pm; lunch time concerts on first Mon of month except Aug; charge). It was built by Inigo Jones for James I as part of Whitehall Palace in 1619–22 and was

probably London's first building made of Portland stone, and first in the classically influenced style of the 16th-century Italian architect Andrea Palladio. It must have looked astonishingly avant-garde among the Tudor timber-and-brick buildings surrounding it (these burnt down in 1698).

Inside, the Rubens ceiling provides a robust contrast to the restraint of the exterior. Commissioned by Charles I to glorify his father James I, it celebrates the divine right of the Stuart kings. However, a bust over the entrance commemorates the fact that Charles was beheaded just outside in 1649.

Downing Street

On the opposite side of the road, and further along, is **Downing Street ❻**, home to the prime minister of the day since 1732. Traditionally, the prime minister lives at No. 10, and the chancellor at No. 11. Since 1989, steel gates have closed the street to the public for security reasons.

PARLIAMENT SQUARE

Now continue down Whitehall, passing, on your right, the **Foreign Office**, designed by George Gilbert Scott in Italianate style and completed in 1868, before coming to Parliament Square.

On your left is the **Palace of Westminster ❼**, where the two Houses of Parliament (the House of Lords and the House of Commons) meet. Visitors can attend debates, watch judicial hearings and committees, and take guided tours of the building (general informa-

tion: tel: 020-7219 4272; tours: tel: 0870 906 3773; www.parliament.uk; charge). Tickets may sometimes be available on the day from the office next to the Jewel Tower in Old Palace Yard, opposite.

Monarchs from Edward the Confessor (1003–66) to Henry VIII (1491–1547) have had residences at this location, which is still a royal palace. The oldest part surviving today is Westminster Hall, the walls of which date from 1097; once used as a law court, it was the scene of the trial of the Gunpowder Plot conspirators in 1606. Henry VIII also apparently used it for playing tennis.

The rest of the old palace was almost completely burnt down in a fire in 1834 – the crypt of St Stephen's Chapel and the Jewel Tower survived. Rebuilding took just over 30 years, according to the neo-Gothic plans of Sir Charles Barry and A.W. Pugin.

During World War II, however, a bombing raid destroyed the chamber of the House of Commons, so architect Sir Giles Gilbert Scott was commissioned to design the replacement. Today the vast building contains

nearly 1,200 rooms, 100 staircases and more than 2 miles (3km) of corridors.

Westminster Abbey

Across the road from the Houses of Parliament, on the south side of the square, is **Westminster Abbey** ❽ (tel: 020-7222 5152; www.westminster-abbey.org; main abbey church: Mon, Tue, Thur, Fri 9.30am–4.30pm, Wed 9.30am–7pm, Sat 9.30am–2.30pm; Chapter House and museum: daily 10.30am–4pm; cloisters: daily 8am–6pm; charge). The medieval abbey on

Above from centre: statue of Oliver Cromwell; the neo-Gothic House of Lords.

First UN Assembly West of Parliament Square is the dome of Westminster Central Hall. Now used for conferences and Methodist services, in 1946 it hosted the first assembly of the United Nations. South of the Hall is a good lunch option, see ⑪②.

Big Ben

At the northern end of the Palace of Westminster is the Clock Tower, standing 316ft (96m) tall. It was Pugin's last design before his descent into madness and death. It houses five bells, which strike the Westminster Chimes every quarter hour. The largest of these, which strikes the hour, is Big Ben, the third-heaviest bell in England, weighing 13.76 tonnes. The name 'Big Ben' properly refers only to this bell, but is often used to refer to the whole tower.

The huge clock (the faces are 23ft/7m in diameter) is famous for its reliability. It is fine-tuned with a small stack of old penny coins on its pendulum: adding or removing a penny changes the clock's speed by two fifths of a second per day. UK residents can arrange to climb Big Ben – apply to your MP or a member of the House of Lords. A 20ft (6m) replica, known as Little Ben, stands on a traffic island near Victoria Station.

Food and Drink 🍴
② CINNAMON CLUB
30–2 Great Smith Street; tel: 020-7222 2555; www.cinnamonclub.com; Mon–Fri B, L and D, Sat L and D; £££–££££
More like a colonial club than the Old Westminster Library it once was. The haute cuisine take on Indian cooking is innovative and tasty, and the wines complement the spicy food well.

Above from left:
Westminster Abbey;
member of the Life
Guards; Chelsea
Pensioner in St
James's Park in
spring; ornamental
gate to Green Park
on the Mall.

Tombs of the Great
As well as kings,
Westminster Abbey
became, from early
on, the burial place
of aristocrats and
monks. These
included Geoffrey
Chaucer, who, in the
centuries since, has
gathered around him
kindred spirits (Lord
Tennyson, Thomas
Hardy, etc) to form
Poets' Corner. The
practice was then
extended to others,
including politicians
(Pitt, Gladstone,
Attlee, etc), com-
posers (including
Purcell and Handel)
and scientists (Isaac
Newton, Charles
Darwin, et al).

this site was completed and consecrated in 1065, only a week before Edward the Confessor's death. He, along with almost all monarchs since, was buried here. King Harold and William the Conqueror were subsequently crowned here on St Edward's Chair – again, as have most monarchs since.

Henry III rebuilt the abbey in the 13th century, and only the Pyx chamber (royal treasury) and undercroft remain of the original. The fan-vaulted Henry VII Chapel was added from 1503 to 1512, and architect Nicholas Hawks-moor built the west towers in 1745.

Among the church's many relics and monuments *(see left)* is St Edward the Confessor's burial vault, rediscovered in 2005 beneath the mosaic pavement, before the High Altar. Also of note is the Chapter House, with its fine 13th-century tiled pavement, and, further on, the Little Cloister and College Garden.

St Margaret's

Next door is the official church of the House of Commons, **St Margaret's** **9** (tel: 020-7654 4840; Mon–Fri 9.30am–4.30pm, Wed until 7pm, Sat 9.30am–2.30pm; free). Inside, the fine east window (1526) commemorates the marriage of Henry VIII and Catherine of Aragon, while the west window (1888) is a tribute to Sir Walter Raleigh (1552–1618), executed for treason nearby. He is buried in the chancel.

Cabinet War Rooms

Leaving Parliament Square by Great George Street, you come to the edge of St James's Park. Turn right, and on the

corner of King Charles Street are the **Churchill War Rooms** **10** (tel: 020-79 30 6961; cwr.iwm.org.uk; daily 9.30am–6pm; charge), the underground bunker from which Winston Churchill master-minded his World War II campaign.

Little has changed since it was closed on 16 August 1945; every book, map, chart and pin remains in place, as does the BBC microphone Churchill used for his famous wartime broadcasts. There is even a telephone scrambler system, concealed as a lavatory; this gave the prime minister a hotline to the White House. A museum displays the great man's red velvet romper suit, bowler hat, champagne and cigars.

ST JAMES'S PARK

Now stroll into **St James's Park** **11** (tel: 020-7298 2000; www.royalparks.org. uk; daily 5am–midnight; free). Henry VIII first formed it by draining a swamp; Charles II decked it out in French style with a straight canal; and George IV, with architect John Nash, put a bend in the lake, gave it an island and also a bridge with some of the best views in London. Today, the park is a favourite lunching spot for civil ser-vants from nearby government offices – if you are peckish too, consider stop-ping at **Inn the Park**, see **①③**.

THE MALL

Emerging from the park on its northern perimeter, you find yourself on the pink tarmac of The Mall, the processional route running from Aston Webb's

Admiralty Arch (1912) to his **Queen Victoria Memorial** (1911) in front of Buckingham Palace. The road was originally laid out by Charles II when he wanted a new pitch for *pallemaille* (Pall Mall, his favourite pitch, had become too crowded). This was a popular game of the time, and involved hitting a ball through a hoop at the end of a long alley.

Carlton House Terrace

Almost opposite where Horse Guards Road joins The Mall, is a grand staircase leading up to Nash's **Carlton House Terrace** ⓬. This complex, completed in 1835, was built on the site of the recently demolished mansion of the Prince Regent (later George IV; *see p.48*), who had decided to move to a revamped Buckingham House (later Buckingham Palace).

The enormous column in between the two sections of terrace is a tribute to 'The Grand Old Duke of York' of the children's nursery rhyme. The duke was in fact commander-in-chief during the French Revolutionary Wars. The memorial was paid for by stopping a day's pay from all ranks of the army.

ICA

Tucked under Carlton House Terrace on the Mall is the **Institute of Contemporary Arts** ⓭ (tel: 020-7930 3647; www.ica.org.uk; Wed–Sun noon–late; charge), with a gallery, cinema, bar-restaurant (see ⓲④) and bookshop. It was founded in 1948 by art critic Herbert Read, with a remit to challenge traditional notions of art.

St James's Palace

Walking down The Mall towards Buckingham Palace, on your right you pass the garden walls of **Marlborough House**, built by Christopher Wren from 1709 to 1711. It was the home of Queen Mary, grandmother of the present Queen, until her death in 1953. Adjacent, on Marlborough Road, is the Queen's Chapel, designed by Inigo Jones; its interior can be viewed during Sunday services, from Easter to July.

Next on your right is **St James's Palace** ⓮ (closed to the public). This castellated brick building was commissioned by Henry VIII, but only became the principal residence of the monarch in London from 1698, when Whitehall Palace burnt down. This is where Mary I died, Elizabeth I waited for the Spanish Armada to sail up the channel, and Charles I spent his final night before being executed. It is now the administrative centre of the monarchy.

Close by is **Clarence House** (access from The Mall; tel: 020-7766 7303; www.royalcollection.org.uk; guided

Guards Museum

On the southern perimeter of St James's Park is Birdcage Walk, where James I once had his aviary, but where you can now visit the Guards Museum (tel: 020-7414 3428; daily 10am–4pm; charge) in Wellington Barracks. It illustrates the history of the British Army's five Guards regiments with uniforms, paintings and medals, and you can even try on a guardsman's bearskin cap. The museum shop sells toy soldiers.

Food and Drink 🍴

③ INN THE PARK
Northeast Section of St James's Park; tel: 020-7451 9999; www.peytonandbyrne.co.uk; daily B, L, AT and D; self-service area: £–££; formal restaurant: £££–££££
Features kedgeree or a full English for breakfast, and scones with clotted cream for afternoon tea (when the pelicans are fed outside at 3pm). Self-service snacks also available. Service can be slow.

④ ICA BAR
12 Carlton House Terrace (entrance on The Mall); tel: 020-7930 0493; www.ica.org.uk; Wed–Sun L and D; ££
The bar attracts a lively, arty crowd. Food, served till late, includes good burgers, enchiladas and salads.

Above from left:
Changing the Guard outside Buckingham Palace; Botticelli's *Venus and Mars* (c.1485), one of the highlights of the National Gallery.

The Royal Mews
Visit the Royal Mews on Buckingham Palace Road (late Mar–Oct daily 10am–5pm, Nov–mid-Dec 10am–4pm; charge) to see the Queen's horses, carriages and motor cars used for coronations, state visits, weddings and other events. You can see the Coronation Coach, built for George III in 1762, visit the stables of the horses (mainly Cleveland Bays and Windsor Greys) and admire the footmen's lavish costumes.

tours Aug Mon–Fri 10am–4pm, Sat–Sun 10am–5.30pm; charge), the residence of Prince Charles, and formerly (1953–2002), the home of the Queen Mother, whose art collection and mementoes are still in place.

BUCKINGHAM PALACE

Now, continue to the forecourt of **Buckingham Palace ⑮** (tel: 020-7766 7300; www.royalcollection.org.uk; State Rooms late July–Sept daily 9.30am–6.30pm; buying tickets in advance online strongly advised; charge). Originally the country house of the Duke of Buckingham (hence the name), the building was bought in 1761 by George III for his wife, Queen Charlotte. George IV came to the throne in 1820 and had the mansion transformed into a palace by the architect John Nash. By 1829, however, the costs had risen to £500,000, and Nash was replaced by Edward Blore to finish the work.

On completion, the first monarch to move in was Queen Victoria, in 1837. Remarkably, she soon found there were no nurseries and too few bedrooms, so a fourth wing was built. The palace finally arrived at its present state in 1914, when the facade was redesigned by Sir Aston Webb.

In front of the Palace, Changing the Guard takes place daily, as at Horse Guards (www.changing-the-guard. com; May–July daily at 11.30am; Aug–April alternate days at 11.30am, see website for details; free). Here, the ceremony is accompanied by music from the Guards' band and takes 40 minutes.

The State Rooms
The Palace has 775 rooms, including 52 royal and guest bedrooms, 188 staff bedrooms and 78 bathrooms. In summer, when the Queen stays at Balmoral Castle in Scotland, the State Rooms (used regularly by the Queen for state banquets, receptions and ceremonies) are open to the public. The sumptuous interiors feature paintings by Rembrandt, Vermeer, Poussin and Canaletto, as well as fine sculpture and furniture.

Queen's Gallery
Further along Buckingham Palace Road from the entrance to the State Rooms is the **Queen's Gallery** (tel: 020-7766 7301; daily 10am–5.30pm; charge). This displays selections from the royal art collection, including numerous royal portraits (notably by Holbein and Van Dyck), paintings by Rembrandt, Rubens and Canaletto, and drawings by Leonardo, Holbein, Raphael, Michelangelo and Poussin.

From here the nearest tube is at Victoria, southwest down Buckingham Palace Road. For the **Vincent Rooms**, see ⑪⑤, head down Buckingham Gate, Artillery Row and Rochester Road.

Food and Drink 🍴
⑤ THE VINCENT ROOMS
Westminster Kingsway College, Vincent Square; tel: 020-7802 8391; www.thevincentrooms.com; Mon–Fri L and D; ££–£££
Britain's top catering college (where Jamie Oliver trained) serves the day's results to the paying public. Quality ingredients, often superb execution, pleasant surroundings and reasonable prices.

NATIONAL GALLERIES

In a neoclassical building with a 'pepperpot' dome, looking out over Trafalgar Square, is one of the world's finest art collections, displaying about 2,300 masterpieces dating from the mid-13th century to 1900. Adjacent is a gallery devoted to the national collection of portraits.

This tour takes in two of London's most important art galleries, and looks at their collections in detail. The walk can easily be combined with tour 1 *(see p.26)*, which starts at Trafalgar Square.

THE NATIONAL GALLERY

The **National Gallery** ❶ (tel: 020-7747 2885; www.nationalgallery.org.uk; daily 10am–6pm, Fri till 9pm; free) was founded in 1824, when a private collection of 38 paintings was acquired by the British Government for the sum of £57,000 and exhibited in the house of the late owner, banker John Julius Angerstein, at 100 Pall Mall, a modest beginning in contrast with grand institutions such as the Louvre in Paris or Madrid's Prado.

The Move to Trafalgar Square

Before long, a more suitable home for the growing collection was sought. The solution came with William Wilkins' long, low construction, opened in 1834 on the then-recently created Trafalgar Square. From the start, however, the building has been criticised as being somewhat inadequate, and additions ever since have done little to confront the shortcomings.

> **DISTANCE** ½ mile (0.25km) not incl. distance covered in galleries
> **TIME** Half a day
> **START** National Gallery
> **END** National Portrait Gallery
> **POINTS TO NOTE**
> At peak times these galleries can be crowded. Try instead to visit on Sunday mornings, the last few hours on evenings when the galleries open late, or on hot summer weekends, when everyone else is out in the sun. This tour combines easily with walk 1.

The Sainsbury Wing

In 1991 a major extension, the Sainsbury Wing, was built to provide much-needed facilities: new galleries, a lecture theatre, a restaurant, shop and space for temporary exhibitions. It was designed by the postmodern US architect Robert Venturi to harmonise with the rest of the building, while offering a humorous comment on its classical idiom. A previous, more avant-garde proposal had been scrapped after Prince Charles's now-famous denouncement of it as 'a monstrous carbuncle on the face of a much-loved and elegant friend'.

Hidden Treasures

At the outbreak of war in 1939, the National Gallery's paintings were hidden in Manod Quarry in North Wales after Prime Minister Winston Churchill's instructions: 'bury them in caves or in cellars, but not a picture shall leave these islands'.

THE NATIONAL GALLERY

Art Attack

In March 1914 a campaigner for women's suffrage took a knife to Velázquez's *Rokeby Venus*, in protest against the arrest of Emmeline Pankhurst. Later, after another suffragette attacked five Bellini paintings, it was decided to close the gallery until the start of World War I in August, when the Women's Social and Political Union called an end to the protests.

Below: Velázquez's *Rokeby Venus*.

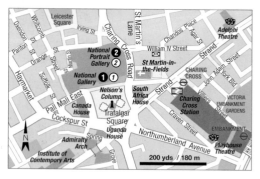

Tour of the Collection

The National Gallery's collection is arranged chronologically, from the 13th century to the end of the 19th, through four wings, starting in the Sainsbury Wing, which contains works from the 13th to 15th centuries. Starting here means resisting the temptation to go into the gallery through its grand main entrance (from where a magnificent staircase offers you a choice of three directions), but it makes sense in terms of the chronology.

Highlights here include medieval and earlier Renaissance works, among them Van Eyck's *The Arnolfini Portrait* (1434), Piero della Francesca's *The Baptism of Christ* (1450s) and the jewel-like *Wilton Diptych* (1395–9) by an unknown artist.

Renaissance Galleries

From the Sainsbury Wing, take the walkway east towards the main building's West Wing and the Renaissance galleries. Here, rooms 2 to 12 display masterpieces of the 16th century, including Raphael's *The Madonna of the Pinks* (1506–7), purchased in 2004 for £22 million; Titian's *Bacchus and Ariadne* (1520–3); and Michelangelo's unfinished *The Entombment* (1500–1).

North Wing

From either room 9 or 14 (in the West Wing), you can access the North Wing, which houses paintings from 1600 to 1700. Here you will find dramatic works by Caravaggio and Rubens, and pensive self-portraits by Rembrandt. Always worth seeking out are Vermeer's quiet and enigmatic *A Young Woman standing at a Virginal* (c.1670–2) and Velázquez's more exuberant *Rokeby Venus* (1647–51), the Spanish painter's only surviving nude.

East Wing

In the East Wing are paintings advancing the story of art from 1700 right up to the threshold of modernity. From the aristocratic portraits of Gainsborough and the rural backwaters of John Constable's landscapes (including *The Hay Wain* of 1821), you soon find yourself, a few rooms on, confronted by the optical innovations of Seurat's *Bathers at Asnières* (1884), the vibrant colours and violent emotions of Van Gogh's *Sunflowers* (1888) and the hints of Cubism in Cézanne's *Bathers* (c.1894–1905).

After all that, you can now recuperate in the Gallery's excellent café immediately below, on Level 0, see 🍴①. Before you leave, don't forget to see the works by Leonardo in room E on the same level, as well as Holbein's *The Ambassadors* (1533) in room C.

NATIONAL PORTRAIT GALLERY

Tucked behind the National Gallery, to the northeast, on St Martin's Place, is the **National Portrait Gallery** ❷ (tel: 020-7306 0055; www.npg.org.uk; daily 10am–6pm, Thur and Fri until 9pm; free except special exhibitions), which is full of famous British faces.

Background
A British historical portrait gallery was founded in 1856, the initiative of the 5th Earl of Stanhope. With no collection as such, it relied on gifts and bequests, the first of which was the 'Chandos' picture of William Shakespeare (*c*.1610), attributed to John Taylor and probably the only portrait of Britain's most famous playwright done from life.

From the start, additions to the collection (initially comprising traditional paintings, drawings and sculpture, with photography added later) were determined by the status of the sitter and historical importance of the portrait, not by their quality as works of art, criteria that still pertain today. Portraits of living people were not admitted until 1968, when the policy was changed to encourage younger artists and a fresh exploration of the genre.

The Collection
The stylish galleries display portraits of important British people past and present. The displays are broadly chronological, starting on the second floor (reached by the vast escalator from the ticket hall) and ending on the ground floor. There are thematic subdivisions within each period: the Tudors and 17th- and 18th-century portraits on the second floor; the Victorians and 20th-century portraits (to 1990) on the first floor; and, on the ground floor, the ever-popular British portraits since 1990 and (usually) excellent temporary exhibitions.

Highlights include self-portraits by Hogarth and Reynolds, Patrick Branwell Brontë's painting of his literary sisters Charlotte, Emily and Anne, and numerous royal portraits. The contemporary galleries have a curiosity value for seeing how today's celebrities are being recorded for posterity.

When you feel sated with art, head up to the third floor for a cocktail or two in the gallery's chic restaurant, see 🍴②.

Food and Drink

① THE NATIONAL CAFÉ
Ground Floor, National Gallery; tel: 020-7747 2525; www.nationalgallery.org.uk; B, L and D: Mon–Fri 8am–11pm, Sat 10am–11pm, Sun 10am–6pm; ££
Waiter-service brasserie, self-service area and espresso bar. Particularly good breakfasts: eggs Benedict, porridge, French toast, etc. Look out for the crisps that are cooked and bagged to order.

② PORTRAIT RESTAURANT
National Portrait Gallery; tel: 020-7312 2490; www.npg.org.uk; daily B and AT, Mon–Fri L, Sat–Sun Br, Thur–Sat D; £££
Fashionable restaurant, lounge and bar with fabulous views over Trafalgar Square. Food is modern British in style.

3

COVENT GARDEN
AND SOHO

East of Charing Cross Road is Covent Garden: once London's fruit and vegetable market, it is now a magnet for shoppers. West of Charing Cross is Soho, which has many excellent restaurants and pubs, as well as a thriving gay scene, Chinatown, plenty of cinemas and plenty of sex shops.

Hanky Panky

In the 18th century Covent Garden was a hotbed of prostitution. Courtesans and madams rented the upper rooms of the elegant houses around the piazza, and punters even had their own guidebook, Jack Harris's *List of Covent Garden Ladies*, which sold over 250,000 copies.

DISTANCE 2 miles (3km)
TIME A full day
START Covent Garden tube
END Leicester Square
POINTS TO NOTE

Note that many shops in central London are open until late on Thursdays (usually until around 8pm), so it may be a good idea to walk the retail-heavy Covent Garden half of this route at that time.

The first half of this walk takes you through the district of Covent Garden. It acquired its name during the reign of King John (1199–1216) as the kitchen garden of Westminster Abbey (or 'Convent') and became a major producer of fruit and vegetables in London for more than three centuries.

In 1540, however, Henry VIII dissolved the country's monasteries, appropriated their land, and formed the Church of England, which, with himself at its head, would be more amenable

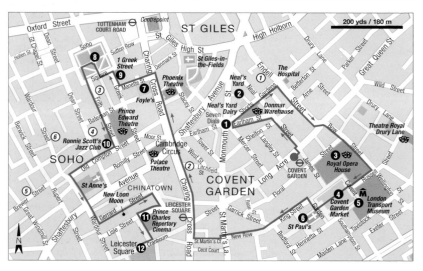

to his frequent changes of wife. Henry granted Covent Garden to Baron Russell, later the first Earl of Bedford.

In the early 17th century, the fourth Earl of Bedford commissioned Inigo Jones to redevelop the area, creating much of the streetplan you see today, as well as the piazza, colonnades and church. Before long a fruit and vegetable market here was thriving, and over the next 250 years, it became the most important in the country.

By the 1970s, though, the congestion of central London had become too much and the market moved south of the river. The 1980s brought a revival, and the district was reinvented as a shopping, eating and tourist hub. Today, the area is equally renowned for its shopping, bars and nightclubs, and eccentric street entertainers.

COVENT GARDEN

From **Covent Garden tube station** (outside which there are always crowds of people) turn right on to Long Acre, lined with high-street chain stores, and then immediately left on to Neal Street, which is full of fashion-forward boutiques. Here, you can buy designer streetwear, natural shoes, baskets, kites, China tea, chic toiletries, handbags and jewellery and the latest trainers.

Turn left on to Earlham Street, where, on your right at No. 41, is the **Donmar Warehouse** (booking tel: 0870 060 6624; www.donmarwarehouse.com), one of London's most innovative theatres. Continue along Earlham Street to the tiny roundabout known as

Seven Dials ❶, the junction of seven streets, then turn right on to Shorts Gardens. At Nos 21–3 is an eccentric water-driven clock above the window of a health food shop; and at No. 17 is Neal's Yard Dairy, an excellent cheese shop. This marks the entrance (on the left) to **Neal's Yard ❷**, which is health-food central – a triangle of shops selling all manner of health foods as well as offering restorative holistic treatments, and with a pleasant Brazilian café.

Continue up Shorts Gardens, across Neal Street again, and turn right on to Endell Street. Just nearby you can pick up some old-fashioned British grub at the acclaimed **Rock & Sole Plaice**, see ⓨ①. Further down Endell Street, on your left at no. 24, is **The Hospital**, a heavily designed art gallery and members' club created by the pop group Eurythmics' Dave Stewart and Microsoft's Paul Allen.

Royal Opera House
Crossing over Long Acre again, you hit Bow Street, home of the 'Bow Street Runners', the forerunners of the police, and the former Magistrates' Court, where Oscar Wilde was convicted in 1895 for committing 'indecent acts'.

Food and Drink ⓨ
① ROCK & SOLE PLAICE

47 Endell Street, Covent Garden; tel: 020-7836 3785; daily L and D; £ London's oldest fish and chip shop (est. 1871). The master-fryer offers the catch of the day (sometimes even mullet or dover sole). Sit inside or out, and if you like, bring your own wine.

Above from far left: interior of Covent Garden Market; ballerinas in action at the Royal Opera House.

Haunted Theatre
From Bow Street, turn left on to Russell Street, and you will find the Theatre Royal Drury Lane on your right. Vulnerable to fire, like the Opera House nearby, this is the fourth theatre to have been built on this site since 1663. With many Georgian features, the ghost-haunted theatre has seen a procession of great names: David Garrick, Sheridan, Kean, Sarah Siddons and Nell Gwynn, the local girl who first sold oranges on opening nights, then became an actress, and finally won King Charles II's heart.

Above from left:
Transport Museum;
British fashion; living
statue in Covent
Garden; market stalls.

Talent Spotting

In *My Fair Lady*
Professor Higgins dis-
covers Eliza Doolittle
selling flowers at
Covent Garden
market while he waits
for a cab home from
the opera. It was also
here that the 15-year-
old Naomi Campbell
was spotted by a
model scout.

Below: Foyle's
bookshop.

Located directly opposite is the
Royal Opera House ❸ (tel: 020-
7304 4000; www.royalopera house.
org; free admission to the Floral Hall,
charge for backstage tours). Now
home to the Royal Opera and Ballet
companies, the theatre was founded
in 1728 with the profits from *The
Beggar's Opera* by John Gay. Since then
it has experienced highs and lows,
from staging premieres of Handel's
operas to being twice burnt down. It
is currently riding high after renovation in the 1990s, and, aside from
performances, you can now have lunch
here, drink in the bar, see exhibitions
and take in views of London's skyline
from the magnificent Floral Hall.

Covent Garden Market

Walking around the side of the Opera
House, down Russell Street, you come
to **Covent Garden Market ❹**. Originally the convent garden of Westminster Abbey, the site came into the
possession of the earls of Bedford, who
commissioned Inigo Jones to design
a new residential estate in the 1630s.
Houses in the terraces facing the
square were set above arcades as in the
elegant rue de Rivoli in Paris, and the
fruit and vegetable market was established here not long afterwards. It
continued until 1974, when it was
moved to Nine Elms on the South
Bank near Vauxhall.

The Covered Market

The market building was redesigned
by Charles Fowler in 1830. In the
North Hall is the Apple Market,
which hosts antiques stalls on Mon-
days, and arts and crafts from Tuesday
to Sunday. Surrounding it are
speciality shops such as Pollock's,
which sells old-fashioned toy theatres
among other amusements. The Punch
& Judy pub nearby is a reminder that
Punch's Puppet Show was first performed here in 1662, as witnessed by
diarist Samuel Pepys.

London Transport Museum

In the southeast corner of the square is
the **London Transport Museum ❺**
(tel: 020-7565 7298; www.ltmuseum.co.
uk; daily 10am–6pm, Fri from 11am;
charge). This child-friendly museum
deals with all aspects of London travel,
from vehicles and uniforms to signs and

posters. Look out in particular for the A Class steam locomotive which hauled passenger trains on the first London Underground line from 1866 until electrification in 1905. There is a shop on the ground floor selling transport related memorabilia.

St Paul's Church

On the western side of the square is **St Paul's ❻** (tel: 020-7836 5221; www.actorschurch.org; Mon–Fri 8.30am–5pm, Sun 9am–1pm; free). In 1631, the earl of Bedford commissioned Inigo Jones to build the church, reportedly on a tight budget, prompting the architect's remark, 'You shall have the handsomest barn in England!' Now known as the 'Actors' Church', for its association with the many theatres in the parish, it contains memorials to Charlie Chaplin, Noël Coward, Vivien Leigh and Gracie Fields.

CHARING CROSS ROAD

Walk down King Street, to the right of the church as you face it, and, at the crossroads, continue on to the partly pedestrianised New Row. When you reach St Martin's Lane (where the ENO is located, *see right*), cross over and walk through St Martin's Court. Then turn right on to Charing Cross Road.

This major road, linking Trafalgar Square with Tottenham Court Road, is traditionally the preserve of London's booksellers. Many have now been forced out by the high rents, but a few remain, including several antiquarian dealers. Try Cecil Court, the next

pedestrianised alley to the south from St Martin's Court, for Hogarth prints, Victorian folding maps of London, vintage theatre posters, modern first editions and sheet music.

Further north on Charing Cross Road is Litchfield Street, on your right, where **Le Beaujolais** is located, see ⑪②. Continuing up past Cambridge Circus, on the left, is **Foyle's** bookshop ❼ (once the world's largest). Then just afterwards is Manette Street, named after Charles Dickens' Dr Manette in *A Tale of Two Cities* and a fitting introduction to Soho, where many French émigrés settled after the Revolution.

SOHO

Bounded by Regent Street, Charing Cross Road, Oxford Street and Leicester Square, Soho embodies the myths of both 1960s 'swinging London' and its more recent, 1990s, ironic version, 'cool Britannia'. Although the maze of narrow streets may not quite live up to the promise of either, there is a definite buzz to the district, helped by the presence of part of London's gay and lesbian scene, as well as a cluster of youthful media companies.

ENO
At the southern end of St Martin's Lane is the Coliseum, home to English National Opera (ENO; tel: 0870-145 0200; www.eno.org). While performances at the Royal Opera House (Covent Garden) are sung in the vernacular, here they are in English. Tickets are cheaper than those at Covent Garden, and can sometimes be bought on the night.

Denmark Street
On the other side of Charing Cross Road from Manette Street is Britain's Tin Pan Alley, where songwriters and music publishers worked in the 1950s and 1960s. The Beatles and Jimi Hendrix made recordings here, Elton John wrote *Your Song*, and the Sex Pistols lived at No. 6. The street is now lined with music stores.

Above from left:
in one of Chinatown's many Chinese restaurants; the legendary jazz venue; Covent Garden and Soho are good for lingerie boutiques; Old Compton Street, the focus of London's gay community.

Before the 17th century, however, this was all open fields, and used as a hunting ground. The first streets to be developed were Old Compton, Gerrard, Frith and Greek streets, laid out in the 1670s by bricklayer Richard Frith.

Today these streets are lined with bars, restaurants and clubs, and remain busy almost around the clock. Despite this being one of London's major nightlife centres, what you see is still a considerably cleaned-up version of the old louche Soho, although there are still remants of a red-light district, tucked away on the quieter streets.

Soho Square and Greek Street

Back at Manette Street, where you entered Soho, turn right into Greek Street and walk up to **Soho Square ❽**. A statue of Charles II shares the square with a ventilation shaft heavily disguised as a half-timbered cottage. Most of the 18th-century houses around the square have been surrendered to television, PR and advertising companies, but **No. 1 Greek Street ❾** (tel: 020-7437 1894; www.hosb.org.uk; guided tours Tue and Thur 9am–11am; charge) has been preserved by a charity for the homeless. Even when the house is closed, its cantilevered 'crinoline' staircase and rococo plasterwork can be glimpsed through the windows.

Frith Street

Now head south from Soho Square via Frith Street. At No. 6, the critic and essayist, William Hazlitt (1778–1830), uttered his last words, 'Well, I've had a happy life,' which should please those staying at the hotel now occupying the building. Opposite is **Arbutus**, see ⑪③, and, beyond, on the corner of Bateman Street, the Dog and Duck pub, with its exuberant Victorian decoration.

Further down, at No. 21, is the house where the paying public came in 1765 to see the nine-year-old Mozart play, thereby replenishing his father's coffers. Opposite, at No. 18, you can test

---

Food and Drink 🍴

③ ARBUTUS

63–4 Frith Street; tel: 020-7734 4545; www.arbutusrestaurant.co.uk; daily L and D, pre-theatre dinners from 5pm; ££
Michelin-starred restaurant that offers remarkable value, especially at lunch time. All the wines, no matter how expensive, are available by the glass or carafe. The modern European dishes are imaginative and tasty. Booking essential.

④ BISTRO DU VIN

36 Dean Street; tel: 020-7490 9230; www.bistroduvinandbar.com; Mon–Sat L and D, Sun D only; ££–£££
This swish restaurant, part of the reputable Hotel du Vin chain, combines comfort and style – there's a long zinc bar, soft banquettes to sink into and booths for a touch of privacy. And the food will warm the cockles of your heart, too. Delicacies such as oysters, Cornish crab and roast bone-marrow are followed by luxurious main courses, from steaks to roasted lobster or bouillabaisse. Alternatively, for a more informal meal, take advantage of the wine-by-the-glass machine and then pay just £12.50 for a platter of charcuterie and fine cheese (in unlimited quantity).

⑤ RANDALL & AUBIN

16 Brewer Street; tel: 020-7287 4447; www.randallandaubin.com; daily L and D; ££
Named after the old delicatessen that inhabited this spot for 90 years, Randall & Aubin has inherited a feeling of shopping bustle. Piles of lobster, crabs and oysters greet you as you enter.

⑥ BUSABA EATHAI

106–10 Wardour Street; tel: 020-7255 8686; www.busaba.com; daily L and D; £–££
Stylishly designed Thai restaurant, with a convivial atmosphere (owing, in part to the communal tables). Serves fresh Thai food at reasonable prices. Good vegetarian options.

your own musical abilities at **Karaoke Box** (tel: 020-7494 3878; www.karaoke box.co.uk). A few doors along at No. 22 is **Bar Italia**, which is open till fashionably late, although otherwise remains impervious to trends. This building is where John Logie Baird gave the first public demonstration of television in 1926.

On the other side of the road, at No. 47, is **Ronnie Scott's Jazz Club** ⑩ (tel: 020-7439 0747; www.ronniescotts.co. uk), where Count Basie played, Ella Fitzgerald sang, and Jimi Hendrix gave his last public appearance.

Around Old Compton Street

At the end of Frith Street, turn right on to Old Compton Street, the focus of Soho's gay scene. If you need a pit-stop at this point, turn right again on to Dean Street for **Bistro du Vin** ⑪④, carry on to the end of Old Compton Street and continue at the crossroads on to Brewer Street and **Randall & Aubin** ⑪⑤, which is sandwiched neatly between sex shops and Italian delicatessens.

Chinatown

Back on Wardour Street, a little to the north, is the popular, dependable **Busaba Eathai**, see ⑪⑥, while, if you follow the street south, across Shaftesbury Avenue, there is the **Wong Kei**, at Nos 41–3, an almost comic multi-storey Chinese restaurant, with famously brusque staff and cheap, yet not so cheerful, food.

Turn left soon afterwards on to **Gerrard Street**, which is Chinatown's main thoroughfare. At No. 9 is the **New Loon Moon supermarket**, in an 18th-century purpose-built brothel. Opposite, at No. 43, is the **New Loon Fung supermarket**, once home to the poet John Dryden (1631–1700).

Leicester Square

At the end of Gerrard Street, turn right at Newport Place, then right again into Lisle Street. Turn left at the excellent **Prince Charles repertory cinema** ⑪ (tel: 0870-811 2559; www. princecharlescinema.com) on Leicester Place to reach **Leicester Square** ⑫. Here, surrounded by the city's largest cinemas – a frequent venue for film premieres – the route ends.

French Connection

In the 17th century the Huguenots started arriving in Soho as religious refugees. Today, there is still a French Protestant Church here, at Nos 8–9 Soho Square. The Roman Catholic French church, on the other hand, is on Leicester Place. Built in the 1950s (its predecessor was bombed in 1940), it has murals by Jean Cocteau and mosaics by Boris Anrep.

Below: retro scooters lined up in Soho.

PICCADILLY AND MAYFAIR

The heart of the West End presents grand thoroughfares, glorious churches and fine art galleries. But beware: you will need your credit card handy for this route, since it takes in some of London's most exclusive shopping streets.

Dracula's House
In Bram Stoker's 1897 novel, *Dracula*, the vampire count buys the house at 347 Piccadilly. Unfortunately, the house numbers do not go up that high, and the address is a mere fiction.

DISTANCE 2¼ miles (3.5km)
TIME Half to a full day
START Piccadilly Circus
END Oxford Street
POINTS TO NOTE

If you are merely interested in taking in the sights, this route could comfortably be completed in half a day. If, on the other hand, you are a keen shopper, the time scale could extend indefinitely, as you shop between sights.

Not for nothing is Mayfair the most expensive square on the London Monopoly board. This is the area for five-star hotels, art dealers, Bentley showrooms, offices of hedge funds and haute couture stores. Running east–west on its southern edge is Piccadilly (smart St James's is to the south), while Oxford Street, the capital's high street, runs along the north boundary. On the western border is Park Lane (the second most expensive square on the Monopoly board).

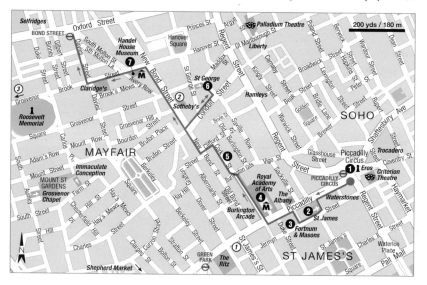

Regent Street

Forming the eastern boundary of Mayfair, curving northwards from Piccadilly Circus, is **Regent Street**, Britain's first purpose-built shopping street, designed by John Nash and completed in 1825. It was built to link the future George IV's residence at Carlton House in St James's to Regent's Park, and is still part of the Crown Estate today. Although the present route will take you down Piccadilly itself, worthwhile destinations on Regent Street for another time include the toyshop Hamley's, Art Nouveau Liberty & Co., and the BBC's Broadcasting House, beyond Oxford Street.

PICCADILLY CIRCUS

Coming out of Piccadilly tube station, you enter the melée of **Piccadilly Circus ❶**. Above are the famous neon billboards; the first electric advertisements appeared here in 1910.

The porticoed building on the north-eastern side of the circus, the **London Pavilion**, was built as a music hall in 1859; sadly today it is a rather uninspiring shopping centre. On the south side is the more appealing **Criterion Theatre**, designed by Thomas Verity and opened in 1874; after refurbishment, it is once again putting on plays.

Eros

In the centre of the circus is a fountain topped with a statue known as **Eros**. It was erected in 1892–3 to commemorate Lord Shaftesbury, a Victorian politician who campaigned for better conditions in factories and coal

mines, for mental health provision and child welfare. Despite its name, the aluminium statue is actually of Eros's twin, Anteros. The sculptor Alfred Gilbert chose Anteros as the embodiment of selfless love, using a 16-year-old Italian boy as his model.

PICCADILLY

Leaving Piccadilly Circus, walk along Piccadilly. The street's name is thought to have come from 'piccadill', the stiff collars you see in portraits of Elizabeth I or Sir Walter Raleigh, and made by a 17th-century local tailor, Robert Baker. On the south side of the street, in a fine Art Deco building, is the flagship branch of Waterstone's, supposedly the largest bookshop in Europe.

St James Piccadilly

A little further down is the church of **St James Piccadilly ❷** (tel: 020-7734 4511; www.st-james-piccadilly.org; daily; free), designed by Christopher Wren and consecrated in 1684. Seek out the carved work of Grinling Gibbons: the fine limewood reredos and the marble font (in which the poet William Blake was baptised).

Shopping

Directly behind the church is **Jermyn Street**, lined with London's finest shirtmakers and gentlemen's outfitters. Take a look there before returning to Piccadilly, where the next stretch of the road offers other interesting shopping opportunities. At No. 187 is the bookshop **Hatchard's**, which has operated

Above from far left:
elegant Berkeley
Square; bespoke
tailoring; Eros;
teddies at Hamley's.

The Albany
Next to the Royal Academy is a fine mansion built from 1770–4 to designs by Sir William Chambers. In 1802 it was converted into chambers for gentlemen, bachelors and those with no connections with trade. Past residents include Lord Palmerston, Gladstone, Byron, Macaulay, the fictional Raffles, Aldous Huxley, Graham Greene, Isaiah Berlin, Terence Stamp, Edward Heath and the diarist Alan Clark.

Above from left:
leather at Mulberry;
truffles at Fortnum
and Mason;
Burlington arcade;
Shepherd Market.

Burlington Arcade
The calm in this up-
market shopping
arcade was shattered
in 1964 when a Jaguar
Mark X sped down it.
Six masked men leapt
out, smashed the
windows of the
Goldsmiths and
Silversmiths
Association shop, and
stole jewellery valued
at £35,000. They
were never caught.

on this site since 1801. The young
Noël Coward was caught shoplifting
here in 1917, packing books into a
stolen suitcase. A few doors down is
Fortnum and Mason ❸, grocers to
the royal family. Even if you do not
want to buy anything it is worth popping in to see its beautifully preserved
Edwardian interior. Further along again
is another gorgeous interior, this time
a restaurant, the **Wolseley** ⑪①, open
for refreshment at any time of day.

Royal Academy of Arts
On the opposite side of Piccadilly is
Burlington House, home of the **Royal
Academy of Arts** ❹ (tel: 020-7300
8000; www.royalacademy.org.uk; daily

10am–6pm, Fri until 10pm; charge),
founded in 1768. A statue of its first
president, the painter Joshua Reynolds,
can be seen in the front courtyard. The
Academy's main function today is the
staging of large exhibitions of great art
from the past. There is also an annual
summer exhibition of new art, to which
anyone can submit pictures for inclu-
sion; the best are selected and are
available for purchase.

From the Royal Academy, walk
through Burlington Arcade, just adjacent on the west side. Watch out for the
'Beadles', guards who patrol this haven
of luxury boutiques in their traditional
uniforms of top hats and tailcoats.

MAYFAIR

Emerging from the arcade you will
find yourself on Burlington Gardens,
in Mayfair. Off to the right is Savile
Row, where bespoke tailors create the
finest men's suits in the world, while to
the left are the fashion emporia of
exclusive Bond Street. Immediately in
front of you, however, is Cork Street.

Commercial Art Galleries
Cork Street ❺ is one of the places in
London (others include Dover Street,
Dering Street and Bond Street, all
nearby), where the top art dealers
cluster. Major galleries on this street
include Bernard Jacobson at No. 6 and
Waddington Custot at No. 11. Among
the most successful artists represented
here are Frank Stella, Robert Indiana,
Peter Blake, Ben Nicholson and
Howard Hodgkin.

Food and Drink 🍴

① THE WOLSELEY
160 Piccadilly; tel: 020-7499 6996; www.thewolseley.com; daily
B, L, AT and D; £££
This place was built as a car showroom in 1921, converted into
a posh branch of Barclay's Bank in 1927, then a restaurant in
2003. The interior is exceptional, and the breakfasts (including
omelette Arnold Bennett – made with haddock, mustard and
cheese), all-day menu for snacks (even steak tartare) and afternoon tea (nice cakes) are delicious. Lunch and dinner are also
good, but booking is advisable.

② SOTHEBY'S CAFÉ
34–5 New Bond Street; tel: 020-7293 5077; www.sothebys.com;
B, L and AT; ££
For a reasonable-value breakfast, lunch and afternoon tea in an
expensive neighbourhood, bear in mind the surprisingly unstuffy
café on the ground floor of this venerable auction house.

③ LE GAVROCHE
43 Upper Brook Street, Mayfair; tel: 020-7408 0881; www.le-
gavroche.co.uk; Mon–Fri L and D, Sat D only; ££££
Chef Michel Roux Jr offers haute cuisine in the grand style, and
the three-course set lunch at £51, including half a bottle of wine
per person, coffee and water, is a bargain. Undoubtedly one of
London's best restaurants.

Bond Street

At the end of Cork Street turn left on to **Bond Street**, where you will find exclusive couturiers and designer boutiques (Chanel, Gucci, Prada, *et al*), jewellers (Asprey, Boucheron, Bulgari), as well as art and antiques galleries. The southern half of the street is the more upmarket. At Nos 34–5 is the headquarters of **Sotheby's**, the famous auctioneers founded in 1744. Members of the public are free to enter and watch an auction or view the items for sale. There is also an excellent café, see ⑪②.

Walking north up Bond Street, a short detour off to the right on Maddox Street brings you to **St George's Church** ❻ (tel: 020-7629 0874; www. stgeorgeshanoversquare.org; Mon–Fri 8am–4pm, Sun 8am–noon; free). When it was first built, George Frederick Handel was a regular worshipper here; much later, it was the venue for the weddings of George Eliot (1880) and Teddy Roosevelt (1886).

Brook Street

Back on Bond Street, further up and off to the left is Brook Street. At No. 25, among more luxury goods shops, is the **Handel House Museum** ❼ (tel: 020-7495 1685; www.handelhouse. org; Tue–Sat 10am–6pm, until 8pm Thur, Sun noon–6pm; charge), where the composer of *The Messiah* lived from 1723 until his death in 1759. Next door, much later (1968–9), lived a very different musician – Jimi Hendrix – commemorated by a blue plaque.

Further up Brook Street is **Claridge's**, one of the city's smartest hotels.

Chef Gordon Ramsay runs the hotel restaurant, and it is much easier to get a reservation here than for his flagship Chelsea restaurant. Perhaps even better, though, is **Le Gavroche**, see ⑪③, further up still, on Upper Brook Street.

Oxford Street

Turning north up Davies Street (opposite Claridge's) you emerge on **Oxford Street**, where, as well as souvenir shops, there are big department stores – notably Selfridges, John Lewis and House of Fraser. When you have had enough shopping, escape via one of the tube stations: going from west to east, Marble Arch, Bond Street, Oxford Circus or Tottenham Court Road.

Shepherd Market

Off Piccadilly, down White Horse Street, is this pretty square with a clutch of good pubs and places to eat outdoors (especially L'Artiste Musclé, at 1 Shepherd Market). This used to be the scene of the annual May Fair (after which the district is named), held here from 1686 until 1764, when it was banned in this location because of riotous behaviour.

Below: bright lights at The Ritz.

MARYLEBONE

In contrast to hectic, overtly commercial Oxford Street to the south, elegant Marylebone exudes a calm villagey air. This walk takes you along its main artery, with art, waxworks and Victorian sleuthing along the way.

DISTANCE 1¼ miles (2km)
TIME Half a day
START Bond Street tube
END Baker Street
POINTS TO NOTE
Visit Madame Tussauds after 5pm to reduce the price and queuing time. Do the walk on Sunday if you want to visit Moxon Street's farmers' market.

Wigmore Hall
On the north side of Wigmore Street is the Art Nouveau Wigmore Hall (booking tel: 020-7935 2141; www.wigmore-hall.org.uk), erected in 1901 as a venue for recitals of classical chamber music. The concerts at 11.30am every Sunday are popular, and breakfast in the café downstairs is an equally big draw.

The need to relieve congestion in Oxford Street in the early 18th century inspired the building of a new road from Paddington to Islington through the parish of St Mary-by-the-bourne. The wealthy Portman family funded the development of the adjacent district: Marylebone (pronounced 'marry-le-bun'), which retains its genteel ambience and many of its Georgian buildings.

ST CHRISTOPHER'S PLACE

From **Bond Street** tube, cross to the other side of Oxford Street and walk north up narrow **St Christopher's Place ❶**, a pedestrian enclave full of boutiques and cafés, including **Carluccio's**, see ⓜ①.

North of St Christopher's Place is Wigmore Street, where medical specialists spill over from nearby Harley and Wimpole streets, the domains of private physicians since the 1840s.

WALLACE COLLECTION

Turn left on Wigmore Street, then second right on to Duke Street, which leads to Manchester Square. On the far side of the square is Hertford House and the **Wallace Collection ❷** (tel: 020-7563 9500; www.wallacecollection.org; daily 10am–5pm; free).

Bequeathed to the British nation by the widow of Richard Wallace, the illegitimate son of the fourth Marquess of Hertford, the collection comprises paintings, furniture, porcelain and a

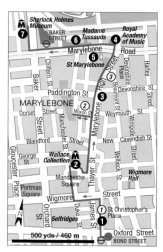

surprisingly large quantity of armour. Highlights include works by Boucher, Fragonard, Watteau, Franz Hals (notably his *Laughing Cavalier)*, Rembrandt and Rubens. The gallery has a restaurant in the glazed-over courtyard.

THE HIGH STREET

Turn left as you leave the gallery and take Hinde Street east off the square. Turn left at the crossroads and walk up Thayer Street, which becomes **Marylebone High Street ❸**. This strip has the feel of a well-heeled urban village, with chic boutiques, bookstores (the Oxfam Bookshop and Daunt Books), gourmet delicatessens and hip cafés.

Halfway up, on the left, is Moxon Street and **La Fromagerie**, see ⑪②; on Sunday a farmers' market is held here (10am–2pm). Back on the high street, at No. 55, is the Conran Shop and the **Orrery** restaurant, see ⑪③ occupying a former stables. Opened in 1999, the shop sparked the area's regeneration and rise to fashionability.

MARYLEBONE ROAD

At the top of Marylebone High Street is the east–west artery, **Marylebone Road**. Straight ahead is the **Royal Academy of Music ❹** (tel: 020-7873 7300; www.ram.ac.uk; museum: Mon–Fri 11.30am–5.30pm, Sat noon– 4pm; free), which hosts concerts and is home to a museum of historic instruments and archive material.

Opposite is **St Marylebone ❺**, the fourth church on this site. The second

was depicted by William Hogarth in his 18th-century *Rake's Progress.*

Madame Tussauds

Walk west at this point for **Madame Tussauds ❻** (tel: 020-7935 6861; www. madame-tussauds.co.uk; July–Sept 9am–5.30pm, Oct–June 10am–5.30pm; charge). Expect to queue for a while before mingling with and even touching the wax and silicone doppelgängers, some more convincing than others. The stress is on contemporary celebrities and bizarre special effects.

BAKER STREET

Now continue further west for Baker Street. At No. 239 is the **Sherlock Holmes Museum ❼** (tel: 020-7935 8866; www.sherlock-holmes.co.uk; daily 9.30am–6pm; charge), which recreates the home of Sir Arthur Conan Doyle's fictional super-sleuth.

Madame Tussaud Marie Grosholtz prepared death masks of victims of the French Revolution of 1789. She left her husband, François Tussaud, in 1802 to spend 33 years touring Britain with a growing collection of wax figures. The current museum dates to 1884.

Food and Drink ⑪

① CARLUCCIO'S
St Christopher's Place; tel: 020-7935 5927; www.carluccios.com; daily B, L and D; ££
Antonio Carluccio's flagship 'caffè'-cum-deli makes the most of the location with attractive outdoor seating. Light, fresh Italian fare.

② LA FROMAGERIE
2–4 Moxon Street; tel: 020-7935 0341; www.lafromagerie.co.uk; daily B, L, AT and pre-theatre D; ££–£££
The café at the back of this up-market cheese shop does inventive salads, wholesome soups and fine cheese plates.

③ ORRERY
55 Marylebone High Street; tel: 020-7616 8000; www.orrery-restaurant.co.uk; daily L and D; £££
Intensely flavoured dishes, a good wine list and an excellent cheese trolley are found in this elegant Conran restaurant.

6

REGENT'S PARK

The extravagance of the Prince Regent led to the founding of Regent's Park, worth visiting for its rose gardens, boating lake and zoo, and Regent Street, which linked the park to his old home on The Mall.

Diorama
At 18 Park Square East is the entrance to what was once the Diorama, a three-storey glass-roofed octagonal auditorium (it can be viewed from Peto Place round the corner). Designed by Augustus Pugin senior, it consisted of an auditorium for 200 people, which could be rotated 73 degrees to view either of two stages. Trompe-l'oeil scenes were painted on calico cloths 72ft (22m) high and included Canterbury Cathedral and a Swiss Alpine valley. Special effects were created with music and lighting. Sadly, it was not a great success with the public and closed in 1851.

DISTANCE 2½ miles (4km)
TIME Half to a full day
START Regent's Park tube
END London Zoo
POINTS TO NOTE

For an alternative way to reach the park, take the canal boat from Camden Lock or Little Venice along Regent's Canal. The London Waterbus runs regular services in summer (tel: 020-7482 2660; www.londonwaterbus.com); reduced service in winter.

Regent's Park (tel: 020-7486 7905; www.royalparks.org.uk; daily 5am–dusk; free) was originally part of Henry VIII's hunting chase around London. It began to take on its current form in 1811, when the Prince Regent (1762–1830), the future George IV, took control and hired John Nash as architect. Of Nash's original scheme, not everything was realised: his summer palace was never built, and only eight of 56 villas for the Prince's friends were erected (two survive); however, his terraces, churches, barracks and river were all put in place.

The park became home to the Zoological, Royal Toxophilite (archery) and Royal Botanic societies, and opened to the public in 1835. A century later Queen Mary's Gardens were added.

NASH'S TERRACES

Emerging from **Regent's Park tube station** at the centre point of Nash's Park Crescent, fortify yourself with breakfast or lunch at the RIBA Café, see ⑪① (Portland Place is due south and on the left). Walk back up again and cross the busy road to Park Square East, where formerly you would have entered the **Diorama ❶** *(see left)*. At the square's northeast corner is St Andrew's Place, dominated by the Royal College of Physicians, the arch-modern masterpiece – completed in 1964 – of architect Denys Lasdun.

Walk up the Outer Circle past **Cambridge Gate ❷**, built in 1880 on the site of the Colosseum – a domed building designed by Decimus Burton in 1827, which housed a panorama of London painted on 40,000 sq ft (3,716 sq m) of canvas; it did not attract enough visitors and was demolished in 1875.

Next along is patrician Chester Terrace: walk through the middle of this via **Chester Gate ❸**. To the right of the archway is a small villa and, mounted on the wall, the bust of a man with 'round head, snub nose, and little eyes' – Nash's description of himself. Emerging from the archway at the end of the terrace, turn left and cross over the Outer Circle to enter the park.

QUEEN MARY'S GARDENS

Follow the path straight on into the park until you reach **Broad Walk**, lined with benches. Turn right for the **Honest Sausage**, see ①②. Turn left, then right on Chester Road, for the **Inner Circle** and **Queen Mary's Gardens ❹**, with 400 varieties of roses, and water gardens, and, on the far side, a café and the open-air theatre (tel: 0870-060 1811; www. openairtheatre.org; summer only).

THE LAKE

Rejoining the Inner Circle at York Gate, walk clockwise round to the path for **Longbridge ❺**, which leads over the lake. This is where Trevor Howard and Celia Johnson went boating in David Lean's romantic cinema classic, *Brief Encounter* (1945). If you think you could do better than Howard, follow the path along the far side of the lake to the **Hanover Bridges ❻**, where boats can be hired (summer 9am–8pm, winter 10am–4pm; charge).

LONDON ZOO

To visit **London Zoo ❼** (tel: 020-7722 3333; www.zsl.org; Mar–Oct daily 10am–5.30pm, Oct–Feb daily 10am–4pm; charge; tickets can be booked online), founded in 1828, take a path north from either Longbridge or the Hanover Bridges. At the Outer Circle turn right for the zoo's main entrance. The zoo is particularly famous for its gorillas, of which there are currently four: Mjukuu, Kesho, Zaire and Effie.

Look out too for the new penguin pool, which opened in 2011. Note that the best time to visit is feeding time, from 2pm.

Above from far left: boating lake and flora in Regent's Park; monkeys at the zoo; Portland Place.

Food and Drink 🍴

① RIBA CAFÉ
66 Portland Place; tel: 020-7631 0467; daily B, L and D; ££
Stylish 1930s setting in the headquarters of the Royal Institute of British Architects. Fresh, light meals.

② THE HONEST SAUSAGE
The Broadwalk, Regent's Park; no tel; www.honestsausage.com; daily 8am–7pm, winter until 4pm; £
This lodge serves high-quality free-range pork sausages from a family-run Gloucestershire butcher in a variety of ways (on mash, in a roll, with an egg, etc); 'guest' sausages sometimes feature. Sausages apart, try the bacon butties, salads, soups and sandwiches (classic fillings such as egg and cress, and cheddar).

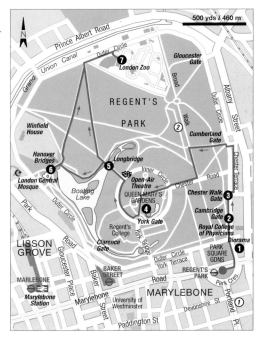

BLOOMSBURY

This is the intellectual part of town. There's the vast British Museum, the homes of Charles Dickens, Virginia Woolf and other literary luminaries, the University of London and a museum of Egyptian archaeology.

Above: bookish cat in literary Bloomsbury.

Tube Station Mosaic
Look out for the brightly coloured mosaics by pop artist Eduardo Paolozzi in Tottenham Court Road station.

DISTANCE 2 miles (3km)
TIME A full day
START British Museum
END Russell Square
POINTS TO NOTE

The nearest tube station to the British Museum is Tottenham Court Road. To reach the starting point from there, leave the tube station via the exit for the Dominion Theatre, walk north up Tottenham Court Road, then turn right into Great Russell Street. Just after the crossroads with Bloomsbury Street, the British Museum is on your left. The museum is vast, so allow at least half a day to explore it.

Food and Drink

① BRITISH MUSEUM CAFÉ
Great Court, British Museum; tel: 020-7323 8990; www.britishmuseum.org; daily B, L and AT; £, Fri D £££
Snacks, sandwiches and drinks in the unique setting of the Great Court, with a magnificent roof by Norman Foster. There is also a smart restaurant upstairs for lunch and afternoon tea daily, plus dinner on Friday.

② TRUCKLES
Pied Bull Yard, off Bury Place; tel: 020-7404 5338; www.davy.co.uk/truckles; Mon–Fri L and D, Sat L only; ££–£££
Traditional Ale and Port House in a courtyard next to the London Review of Books Bookshop. Simple and modern upstairs; candle-lit tables and sawdust-covered floors downstairs; seating outside in summer. Dishes include dressed crab, lamb shank and treacle tart.

Bloomsbury is bounded to the north by Euston, St Pancras and King's Cross railway termini, but this is no typical station hinterland. It is the hotbed of London's intellectual activity: it was home to the Bloomsbury literati of the early 20th century, and still has a distinctly cultural and academic atmosphere, as it is where both the British Museum and the University of London are sited.

BRITISH MUSEUM

The **British Museum** ❶ (tel: 020-7323 8299; www.britishmuseum.org; daily 10am–5.30pm, Fri until 8.30pm; free; short tours of selected exhibits, 30–40 minutes, available daily, free) is one of the oldest museums in the world, founded by an Act of Parliament in 1753 and opened in 1759. It has accumulated a collection of 8 million objects. Devote just 60 seconds to each and you would be there for more than 15 years.

Although only 50,000 objects are on display, this is not a place to rush through in an hour. It is also one of the most visited attractions in London and the best time to go is soon after opening. As there are so many things to see, we cover the highlights below, so that you can prioritise, according to your interest.

Note that options for refreshments in or near the museum include the museum cafe, see Ⓨ①, in the Great Court, redesigned by architect Norman Foster. Alternatively, head for **Truckles**, see Ⓨ②, by leaving the museum, then turning left, crossing over and taking a right turn on to Bury Place; Truckles is in a courtyard just on your left.

Egyptian Mummies: Rooms 62–3
By far the biggest crowd-puller in the museum are the Egyptian sarcophagi. Thanks to enthusiastic plundering by 19th-century explorers, the collection (located on the upper floor) is the richest outside Egypt.

Rosetta Stone: Room 4
Another major attraction is the 2nd-century BC granite tablet known as the Rosetta Stone, which provided the key for deciphering Egyptian hieroglyphics. In the same room is the colossal sandstone head of pharaoh Rameses II, said to be the inspiration for *Ozymandias*, Shelley's poem on the transience of power.

Elgin Marbles: Room 18
Among the museum's more controversial holdings are the Elgin Marbles, which represent the high point of ancient Greek art. Carved in the 5th century BC, they depict the battle of the Lapiths and Centaurs, a festival procession for the Goddess Athena, as well as various Greek gods.

The marbles were taken from the Parthenon temple on the Acropolis in Athens by Lord Elgin in the early 19th

century. His action, ironically, saved them for posterity, since the acropolis temples were employed for storing munitions during the Greek War of Independence (1821–33) and much of what remained was reduced to ruin. Understandably, the Greeks want the sculptures returned.

Benin Bronzes: Room 25
In the basement are around five dozen of the 900 brass plaques found in Benin City, Nigeria, in 1897. The Benin Bronzes were probably cast in the 16th century to clad the wooden pillars of the palace; they depict court life and ritual in extraordinary detail.

Anglo-Saxon Ship Burial: Room 41
The Sutton Hoo Ship Burial was the richest treasure ever dug from British soil. The early 7th-century longboat was probably the burial chamber of Raedwald, an East Anglian king. The acidic

Above from far left: the British Museum and some of the ancient Egyptian sarcophagi in its collection.

The Portland Vase
This Roman glass masterpiece (room 70) was made *c*.20BC. In 1845, however, it was smashed by a drunken vandal. Crudely glued back together soon afterwards, it has recently been taken apart again and expertly reassembled. It now looks as good as new.

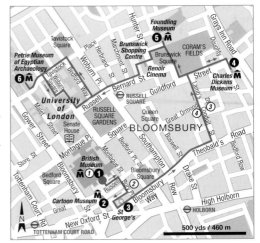

Faber and Faber
T.S. Eliot worked as poetry editor at this famous publisher on Russell Square.

Bloomsbury Group
In the early 20th century, a group of friends, nicknamed the Bloomsberries and including E.M. Forster, Lytton Strachey, J.M. Keynes, Clive and Vanessa Bell, Duncan Grant and Virginia and Leonard Woolf would meet at each other's houses at Nos 37, 46, 50 and 51 Gordon Square to discuss literature and art. Other notable Bloomsbury residents have included Thomas Carlyle at 38 Ampton Street, Edgar Allan Poe at 83 Southampton Row, Anthony Trollope at 6 Store Street and W.B. Yeats at 5 Upper Woburn Place.

sand had destroyed all organic material well before the excavation in 1939, but a rich hoard of weapons, armour, coins, bowls and jewellery survived.

Other Highlights
In room 40 are the Lewis Chessmen, found on the Isle of Lewis in Scotland's Outer Hebrides and probably made in Norway. These 12th-century chess pieces are elaborately carved from walrus ivory and whales' teeth, The helmeted figures and faces set in curious scowls are almost comical.

Room 50 exhibits the preserved corpse of Lindow Man, the victim of a sacrifice, who was found in a peat bog in Cheshire in 1984. Scientists were able to determine his blood group, what he looked like and what he had eaten.

HISTORIC STREETS

When you are finished at the museum, walk down Bury Place and turn right at Little Russell Street. Follow this road across Museum Street to stop at the **Cartoon Museum ❷** (tel: 020-7580 8155; www. cartoonmuseum.org; Tue–Sat 10.30am–5.30pm, Sun noon–5.30pm; charge) on your right at No. 35. Alternatively, browse in the bookshops and galleries on Museum Street before continuing the route by turning left on to Bloomsbury Way at the bottom of the street.

Almost immediately on your left is the church of **St George's Bloomsbury** ❸ (tel: 020-7405 3044; www.stgeorges bloomsbury.org.uk; Mon 1–4pm, Tue–Fri 1–2pm, Sat 11.30am–5pm, Sun

2–5pm; free), the sixth and final London church designed by Nicholas Hawksmoor, the leading architect of the English Baroque. Completed in 1731 it has a steeple in the form of a stepped pyramid surmounted by Britain's only statue of George I.

Continuing along Bloomsbury Way, cross over Southampton Row to Theobald's Road. The fifth turning on your left is Lamb's Conduit Street, full of shops, historic pubs, cafés and restaurants, including **Cigala** and **Vat's Winebar**, see ⑪③ and ⑪④. Continue to the end of the street, then turn right at Guildford Place and right again on to Doughty Street.

DICKENS MUSEUM

At 48 Doughty Street is the **Charles Dickens Museum ❹** (tel: 020-7405 2127; www.dickensmuseum.com; daily 10am–5pm; charge). The author lived here from 1837–9 while writing *Nicholas Nickleby* and *Oliver Twist*. It is the only one of his London homes still standing, and exhibits all manner of memorabilia: his letters, manuscripts, desk, locks of his hair and even his lemon squeezer.

FOUNDLING MUSEUM

Retrace your steps to Guildford Place, where, on your right, is **Coram's Fields**, a children's park (adults admitted only with a child). Facing on to the park on the west side at 40 Brunswick Square is the **Foundling Museum ❺** (tel: 020-7841 3600; www.foundlingmuseum.

org.uk; Tue–Sat 10am–5pm, Sun 11am–5pm; charge). Formerly Thomas Coram's Foundling Hospital, it cared for 27,000 abandoned children between 1739 and 1953, when it closed.

As well as telling the hospital's story – with poignant mementoes left by mothers for their babies – the museum has important collections relating to two of its first governors, the artist William Hogarth and the composer George Frederick Handel. Hogarth encouraged artists of the day to donate works and, in doing so, created Britain's first public art gallery. The collection includes works by Hogarth, Reynolds and Gainsborough, displayed in the original interiors.

Handel donated proceeds from annual performances of *The Messiah* and bequeathed the manuscripts to the hospital. The museum has since acquired a huge collection relating to Handel, including manuscripts, books and music, libretti and paintings.

UNIVERSITY OF LONDON

Leaving the Foundling Museum, head for the other side of the square and the Futurist-inspired Brunswick Centre, designed by Patrick Hodgkinson in 1973 and recently given a much-needed face-lift. Walk up the steps by the Renoir arts cinema and turn left through the complex past the cafés and restaurants to emerge on Bernard Street. Walk past the tube station and on to Russell Square. Turn right off the square on Bedford Way and you are in university territory.

At the end of the street, turn left and walk along the south side of Gordon Square. Blue plaques on the houses here commemorate the residences of various members of the Bloomsbury Group. Economist J.M. Keynes lived at No. 46 and Lytton Strachey at No. 51. Continuing west of the square on to Byng Place, look out on your right for Malet Place, an inconspicuous lane that leads into University College and the **Petrie Museum of Egyptian Archaeology** ❻ (tel: 020-7679 2884; www. petrie.ucl.ac.uk; Tue–Sat 1–5pm; free). Inside, look for the world's oldest dress (2800BC).

Finally, return to Russell Square, and the tube, by turning right off Gordon Square, cutting through Woburn Square and turning left.

Food and Drink 🍴

③ CIGALA
54 Lamb's Conduit Street; tel: 020-7405 1717; www.cigala.co.uk; L and D daily; £££
Buzzing Spanish neighbourhood restaurant offering tapas or à la carte dishes under the aegis of owner-chef Jake Hodges (ex-Moro in Clerkenwell). Excellent sherries, wines and liqueurs. Good-value set lunch menus.

④ VAT'S WINEBAR
51 Lamb's Conduit Street; tel: 020-7242 8963; www.vatswinebar.com; Mon–Fri L and D; £££
Well-established and perennially popular wine bar. In a comfortable wood-panelled interior, the friendly staff serve comforting food to accompany the serious wine list. Expect hearty portions of pork belly, pheasant casserole and lamb shank.

University Library
In World War II, the Senate House Library on Russell Square was used as the Ministry of Information. Hitler then earmarked it for his post-invasion HQ. It was also the model for the Ministry of Truth in George Orwell's *1984*.

Wellcome Collection
North of the university, opposite Euston Station, is the excellent Wellcome Collection (183 Euston Road, www.wellcome collection.org; Tue–Sun 10am–6pm, Thur until 10pm; free), a museum/art space devoted to medicine and its relationships with art and society. It mixes items from Henry Wellcome's (1853–1936) eclectic collection of objects, interactive exhibits, paintings and more. Other draws include a café and bookshop.

Bowling Alley
Go ten-pin bowling in style in the basement of the Tavistock Hotel on Bedford Way (tel: 020-7691 2610; www.bloomsbury bowling.com). This is a good option for children on a wet day, but note that they are not admitted after 4pm. In the evenings and at weekends it is advisable to book.

HOLBORN AND
THE INNS OF COURT

This area is the domain of journalists and lawyers so vividly described in the novels of Charles Dickens. The atmosphere is well preserved in the winding backstreets, rickety old pubs, quaint shops and historic churches.

Early Printing
Printing and publishing grew up around Fleet Street in the 15th century. The new industry located here because it was an enclave of the clergy: as the clergy had a near monopoly on literacy, they were the printers' best customers.

DISTANCE 2 miles (3km)
TIME Half to a full day
START St Bride's, Fleet Street
END Somerset House
POINTS TO NOTE

The walk may take a whole day if you visit all the museums on the route.
The nearest station to the starting point above is Blackfriars Station (rail and tube). On leaving the station, walk north to reach Fleet Street.
The nearest tube station to Somerset House is Temple on the Embankment.

This tour starts at the western end of Fleet Street, a strip synonymous with print journalism, although the industry has long since moved out. To continue where many a hack left off, set yourself up for the tour with a stop at the **Blackfriar**, see ⑪①, one of the many historic watering holes in this part of London, opposite Blackfriars Station. When sated, walk north to Ludgate Circus, then turn left on to Fleet Street to follow the bank of the old Fleet River, which is now buried in a sewer.

FLEET STREET

On the left, down Bride Lane, rises the steeple of **St Bride's ❶** (tel: 020-7427 0133; www.stbrides.com; Mon–Fri 8am–6pm, Sat 11am–3pm, Sun 10am–6.30pm; free). This church, the inspiration for the first tiered wedding cake, was built by architect Sir Christopher Wren after the Great Fire of London destroyed its medieval predecessor in 1666. Unfortunately, the church was gutted again during the Blitz in 1940, though it has been carefully restored. A museum in the crypt displays Roman mosaics, Saxon church walls as well as a product of England's first printing press, William Caxton's *Ovid*.

Offices of National Newspapers

On the other side of Fleet Street are the former offices of Britain's national newspapers, which relocated in the 1980s to cheaper, high-tech sites such as Wapping in the Docklands. At No. 121 is an Art Deco building of black glass and chromium (nicknamed Black Lubyanka), which was once the nerve-centre of Express Newspapers. A few doors down, the pillared palace at No. 135 used to house *The Telegraph*.

Dr Johnson's House

On the same side of the road, look out for **Ye Olde Cheshire Cheese** pub (rebuilt 1667), once frequented by Samuel Johnson and his cronies, including Oliver Goldsmith, who lived at No. 6. From here it is just a short, well-signposted, walk to **Dr Johnson's House ❷** on Gough Square (tel: 020-7353 3745; www.drjohnsonshouse.org; Mon–Sat 11am–5.30pm, until 5pm in winter; charge). Johnson lived here from 1748 to 1759, compiling his dictionary in the garret with six poor copyists. Outside the house is a statue of Johnson's pet cat, Hodge – 'a very fine cat indeed'.

Returning to Fleet Street, cross the road to **El Vino**, see ⑪②.

Church of St Dunstan-in-the-West

On the other side of Fleet Street, just beyond Fetter Lane, is **St Dunstan-in-the-West ❸** (tel: 020-7405 1929; www.stdunstaninthewest.org; Mon–Fri 11am–2pm; free). It is famous for its 17th-century clock (its two giants strike the hours and quarters), and its association with poet-priest John

Donne, who was rector here (1624–31). Over the porch at the side is a statue of Queen Elizabeth I, the only one known to have been carved during her lifetime.

THE INNS OF COURT

Further along, on the left at No. 17, is the **Inner Temple Gateway**, leading to the quadrangles, chambers and gardens of one of the four Inns of Court. Enter the lane beneath and continue to **Temple Church**, part of which was built in the 1180s for the Knights Templar. Head left across Church Court to King's Bench Walk (where Tony Blair once practised as a barrister) and turn right. Soon, turn right again on to Crown Office Row, and continue past the gardens (Mon–Fri 12.30–3pm; free) to emerge on Middle Temple Lane.

Turn right, passing on your left the buildings of another of the Inns of

Food and Drink 🍴

① BLACKFRIAR PUB

174 Queen Victoria Street, Blackfriars; tel: 020-7236 5474; www.nicholsons pubs.co.uk; daily L and D; ££
The interior of this Victorian pub was remodelled in 1902 by Arts and Crafts exponent, Henry Poole. Every inch is covered in marble, mosaic or low-relief sculpture. Wonderful. Decent real ales, reasonable pub food (until 9pm).

② EL VINO

47 Fleet Street; tel: 020-7353 6786; Mon–Fri B, L and D; ££–£££
Well-established Fleet Street wine bar with convivial atmosphere and hearty food (of the steak and kidney pie school). Good wines. Very fair prices.

Above from far left: classic watering hole El Vino; Samuel Johnson; St Bride's; dragon monument marking the City of London boundary.

Sweeney Todd
Next door to St Dunstan's are the old offices of the *Dundee Courier*, built on the site of Sweeney Todd's barber shop. In the 1780s, Todd is reputed to have killed more than 100 of his clients, and then sold the bodies to Lovett's Pie Shop (in Bell Yard further along) where they were cooked up into meat pies.

Gateway Tavern
On the first floor of the Inner Temple Gateway is Prince Henry's Room (Mon–Fri 11am–2pm), with the initials of James I's son on the elaborate plaster ceiling. The building, which dates from 1611, was originally a tavern called The Prince's Arms.

Above from left: looking out of the historic Seven Stars pub towards the Royal Courts of Justice; view down the Thames, with the City on the right.

Cabbies' Shelter
Turn right at the southern end of Middle Temple Lane and on Temple Place above Embankment is one of the few remaining cabmen's shelters. Once common across London, thanks to the Cabmen's Shelter Fund, set up in 1874, they gave cabbies alternatives to pubs. The green shed was not allowed to take up more space than a horse and cab.

The Silver Vaults
Now home to dealers in fine silver, the London Silver Vaults (www.thesilvervaults. com) at the top of Chancery Lane were opened in 1876 to provide strong rooms for the wealthy to protect their valuables.

Court, **Middle Temple**, and you come out at the point where Fleet Street ends and the Strand begins. This, the boundary of the City of London, is marked by **Temple Bar**, a stone monument topped with a dragon. Further west (in the middle of the road) is the church of **St Clement Danes**, built in 1682 by Sir Christopher Wren. It was damaged in the Blitz but then restored as the church of the Royal Air Force.

Chancery Lane
On the far side of the road are the **Royal Courts of Justice**, where England's most important civil law cases are heard. To its right is Chancery Lane. As you walk up, on your left is Carey Street where you can find wigmakers' shops, the Silver Mousetrap jewellers (est. 1690) and the **Seven Stars** pub, see ①③, the 'Magpie and Stump' of Dickens's *Pickwick Papers*.

Lincoln's Inn Fields
Further up Chancery Lane, enter **Lincoln's Inn** ④ through the arch on the left marked 'New Square'. The more aptly named Old Hall was built during the reign of Henry VII (1485–1509).

Food and Drink 🍽️
③ THE SEVEN STARS
53a Carey Street; tel: 020-7242 8521; daily L and D; ££
Built in 1602, this pub survived the Great Fire, and, thanks to proprietor Roxy Beaujolais, remains unspoilt to this day. Just by the back door of the law courts, it is popular with lawyers. Good beer and food (oysters, herrings, meatloaf, game stew).

Walk straight through to the east gate and **Lincoln's Inn Fields**, London's largest square. On the south side the Royal College of Surgeons houses the **Hunterian Museum** ⑤ (tel: 020-7869 6560; www.rcseng.ac.uk; Tue–Sat 10am–5pm; free) with a collection of fine art, as well as anatomical specimens.

Sir John Soane's Museum
On the north side of the square at No. 13 is the eccentric **Sir John Soane's Museum** ⑥ (tel: 020-7405 2107; www. soane.org; Tue–Sat 10am–5pm and first Tue of month 6–9pm; free). Soane (1753–1826), best known as the architect of the Bank of England, designed this, his own house. Its rooms are just as he left them: packed with antiquities and paintings, including Hogarth's *Rake's Progress* and *The Election*.

Leave the square by the southwest corner, on Portsmouth Street. **The Old Curiosity Shop** from Dickens's novel is on the left (now selling shoes). Navigate the lanes south to reach Aldwych, which leads back to the Strand.

SOMERSET HOUSE

On the south side **Somerset House** ⑦, a Palladian mansion built by Sir William Chambers from 1776–96, is home to the **Courtauld Gallery** (tel: 020-7845 4600; www.courtauld.ac.uk; daily 10am–6pm; charge, Mon until 2pm free), displaying outstanding paintings, from Michelangelo to Monet. In summer, the fountains in the courtyard make way for open-air cinema, while in winter there is an ice rink.

THE CITY

Despite its rich history, the City is no museum. Hi-tech office towers crowd the dome of St Paul's Cathedral, and the Beefeaters at the Tower of London are vastly outnumbered by 300,000 business suits on their daily commute.

The nearest tube to the starting point is Tower Hill. From the tube exit turn right towards the Tower of London. As you walk down the steps of the subway, a section of the old Roman city wall is on your left. On the other side of the road, turn right; the main entrance to the Tower is on the river side.

DISTANCE 2¼ miles (3.5km)
TIME A full day
START Tower of London
END Barbican
POINTS TO NOTE
Walk this route on a weekday, as the City is dormant at weekends.

TOWER OF LONDON

It was in 1078 that William the Conqueror ordered the building of the **Tower of London ❶** (tel: 0844 482 7777; www.hrp.org.uk; Tue–Sat 9am–5.30pm, Sun–Mon 10am–5.30pm; charge). Since then, the most haunted building in England has housed a zoo (from the reign of King John, 1199–1216), a palace (under Henry III, 1216–72) and a VIP prison (inmates included Elizabeth I, Guy Fawkes, Walter Raleigh and briefly, in 1941, Rudolf Hess).

To see the Tower, you might join one of the hour-long tours led by a Yeoman Warder (a Beefeater). Visit the **White Tower**, the only intact Norman keep left in England, and the armoury, which contains an execution axe and chopping block (two of Henry VIII's wives were beheaded here). See also the **Crown Jewels**, stored here since 1303. As well as crowns, orbs and

sceptres, there is a 2m (6½ft) wide punchbowl. Outside, watch out for the Royal Ravens: legend has it that if they ever leave, the Tower will crumble. This came close to happening in World War II, when all but one died from shock during bombing raids.

ALONG THE RIVER

If you are now in need of a rest, cross over Tower Bridge Approach on the eastern side of the Tower of London to **St Katharine's Dock ❷**, where you can enjoy a drink at one of the cafés overlooking the marina. Here, Telford's fine warehouses, once piled with ivory tusks, are the backdrop for Thames barges, restored clippers and an 18th-century warship, *The Grand Turk*.

Now, returning to the main entrance of the Tower, walk up Lower Thames Street, passing **Custom House** (1817) on your left, followed by **Old Billings-**

Tower Bridge
Next to the Tower of London is Tower Bridge (tel: 020-7403 3761; www.tower bridge.org.uk; Apr–Sept 10am–6.30pm, Oct–Mar 9.30am–6pm; charge). Completed in 1894, its iconic 1,000-ton bascules are still raised some 1,000 times a year, though now using electricity and oil rather than steam. The high-level walkways – in their early days popular with prostitutes and pickpockets – offer wonderful views to the paying public. In 1952 a London bus had to leap from one bascule to the other, when the bridge began to rise with the bus still on it.

gate Market, which for centuries had supplied London with fish. Further along, again on the left, is Sir Christopher Wren's church of **St Magnus the Martyr ❸**, completed in 1676 *(see margin, left)*.

THE MONUMENT

London Bridge
St Magnus the Martyr marks the entrance to the original London Bridge, a model of which stands in the vestibule. Old London Bridge, lined with 200 shops, was replaced in 1831 by a simpler granite structure by John Rennie a little upstream. However, the weight caused the foundations to sink, and the bridge was sold in 1968 to an American entrepreneur, who rebuilt it in Arizona. The replacement is practical but bland.

Just before the bridge, turn right up Fish Street Hill to **The Monument ❹** (tel: 020-7626 2717; www.themonument. info; daily 9.30am–5.30pm; charge), a memorial to the Great Fire of 1666, which started in a bakery on Pudding Lane, just nearby. Built by Christopher Wren and Robert Hooke in 1671–7, this 61m (202ft) Doric column was designed to double as a scientific instrument, with a central shaft for use as a zenith telescope (a hinged lid in the flaming urn at the top covers the

opening). Around this shaft wind 311 steps leading up to a cage (added after several suicides) from where you can admire the view.

BANK OF ENGLAND

At the top of Fish Hill Street turn left, and, after the major junction, bear right up King William Street into the financial heart of the City. On the way, you pass Wren's church of **St Clement Eastcheap** on your right (of the nursery rhyme, *Oranges and Lemons*), then Nicholas Hawksmoor's **St Mary Woolnoth**, also on the right. At the end of the street, as you approach the Bank of England, on your left is **Mansion House** *(see margin, left)* and, leading off to the west, Queen Victoria Street where **Sweetings**, see ⑪①, is located. Meanwhile, on the right is the **Royal Exchange**, and Cornhill, leading east to **Simpson's Tavern**, see ⑪②.

On the far side of the junction is Britain's central bank, the **Bank of England ❺** (tel: 020-7601 5545; www. bankofengland.co.uk; Mon–Fri 10am–5pm; free). Designed by architect Sir John Soane in 1788, the building has more space below ground than is contained in the 42 storeys of Tower 42 *(see margin, p.60)*.

Just around the corner on Bartholomew Lane is a **museum** (Mon–Fri 10am–5pm; free) displaying banknotes, gold bars (you can even pick one up), minting machines and examples of firearms that were once issued to bank branches for defence.

Food and Drink ⑪

① SWEETINGS
39 Queen Victoria Street; tel: 020-7248 3062; Mon–Fri L only; ££–£££
This City institution (operating since 1889) specialises in fish. Lunch might involve a pint of Guinness, potted shrimps (with brown bread and butter), smoked haddock (with a poached egg on top) and spotted dick for pudding.

② SIMPSON'S TAVERN
Ball Court, 38 Cornhill; tel: 020-7626 9985; www.simpsonstavern.co.uk; Mon–Fri L only; ££–£££
Down an alley off Cornhill, this time-warped tavern has served hearty pies and stews and puddings (with custard) to old-school-tie-wearing City gents since 1759.

THE GUILDHALL

At the top of Bartholomew Lane, turn left on Lothbury and continue until you reach the City of London's town hall, the **Guildhall** ❻ (tel: 020-7606 3030; www.cityoflondon.gov.uk; phone for times; free). Built from 1411 on the site of a Roman amphitheatre (the outline of the arena is marked in black on the courtyard), this is the only secular stone building to have survived the Great Fire of 1666. Inside is a large medieval hall with stained glass and extensive crypts.

To the rear is the **Guildhall Library**, (tel: 020-7332 1868; Mon–Sat 9.30am–5pm; free), founded in the 1420s with a bequest from Richard Whittington, three times City mayor, and later the inspiration for the pantomime character, Dick. As well as a reference library specialising in London history, it houses the museum of the City clockmakers' guild, displaying more than 600 timepieces.

On the right of the square is the **Guildhall Art Gallery** (tel: 020-7332 3700; Mon–Sat 10am–5pm, Sun noon–4pm; charge). The collection includes Britain's largest painting, *The Siege of Gibraltar* by John Singleton Copley, and Victorian masterpieces by artists such as Millais and Landseer.

ST PAUL'S CATHEDRAL

Now walk down King Street, opposite the Guildhall, and turn on to Cheapside. Coming up on your left is the first of three Wren churches, **St Mary-le-Bow**. Tradition has it that to be a true cockney (East London's old working class), you have to be born within earshot of the sound of the bells. Further along, on your right, is the church of **St Vedast**. Then, on your left, down New Change, is **St Paul's Cathedral** ❼ (tel: 020-7246 8357; www.stpauls.co.uk; Mon–Sat 8.30am–4pm; charge).

College of Arms
South of St Paul's, on the left at the end of Godliman Street, is the College of Arms (tel: 020-7248 2762; tours by arrangement Mon–Fri 6.30pm; charge), which oversees the coats of arms of the nobility.

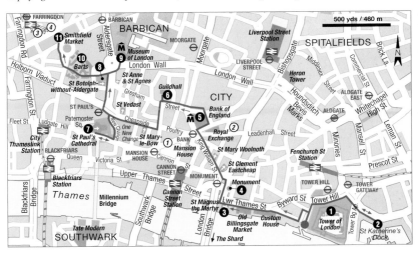

Above from left:
St Paul's, viewed from Ludgate Hill; historic clock by the Royal Exchange; Richard Rogers' Lloyd's Building; Smithfield Market.

City Towers
The tallest building in the City is Tower 42 in Old Broad Street. Designed by Richard Seifert, and built 1971–9, it is 600ft (183m) high. Second is the Gherkin at 30 St Mary Axe (591ft/180m), built by Foster Partners in 2001–4. Third is CityPoint on Ropemaker Street, at 417ft (127m), built in 1967. Towering over all three, however, is The Shard, beside London Bridge station. At 1,017ft (310m) it is the tallest building in the EU.

Pristine white after years of renovation, the cathedral (the fifth on this site) was completed in 1708, on Wren's 76th birthday, after its predecessor was gutted in the Great Fire of 1666. In the later stages of its building, Wren is said to have been hauled up to the rafters in a basket to inspect progress. Inspired by St Peter's Basilica in Rome, the building is centred under a dome rising 108m (354ft) from the floor.

The dome holds three circular galleries. First, up 259 steps, is the Whispering Gallery running around the inside of the dome: whisper against its wall at any point, and your voice is audible to a listener with their ear held to the wall at any other point around the gallery. Oddly, speak at a normal volume, and the sound does not transmit in the same way. The ceiling is decorated with monochrome paintings by Sir James Thornhill of scenes from the life of St Paul. The other two galleries are both outside: the Stone Gallery is 378 steps from ground level, and the Golden Gallery, 530 steps up.

If heights are not your forte, visit the crypt. Christopher Wren was the first to be interred here, in 1723 at the age of 90. Other famous names include the Duke of Wellington and Lord Nelson, the latter having been brought back from the Battle of Trafalgar preserved in a barrel of French brandy.

POSTMAN'S PARK

Return now to New Change, head north, and after the crossroads continue on to St Martin's Le Grand,

which then becomes Aldersgate Street. On your right is Wren's unusual brick church of **St Anne and St Agnes**, based on the plan of a Greek cross.

Opposite, by the church of **St Botolph-without-Aldersgate** (built by George Dance the Elder in 1725) is the **Postman's Park** ❽, the brainchild of painter and philanthropist George Frederick Watts (1817–1904). It was originally a popular lunch time spot for workers from the former General Post Office, nearby. It is now noted for its wall covered in Doulton plaques commemorating fatal acts of bravery by the ordinary people of the Victorian era. One memorial reads, 'Thomas Simpson, died of exhaustion after saving many lives from the breaking ice at Highgate Ponds. Jan 25 1885.'

MUSEUM OF LONDON

Further up Aldersgate Street, past the busy roundabout, is the **Museum of London** ❾ (tel: 0870 444 3851; www. museumoflondon.org.uk; daily 10am–6pm; free). This museum takes you from London's earliest beginnings right up to the late 20th century. Highlights include Roman leather 'bikinis', Viking battle-axes, a hoard of Tudor jewellery, dress and costume, from royal gowns to Norman Hartnell 1920s flapper dresses, paintings by artists from Canaletto to Henry Moore, and the Lord Mayor's gilded coach. There is also a large audiovisual exhibit on the Great Fire, as well as a walk-through Victorian street scene.

BARTS HOSPITAL

From the museum, cross to the other side of the roundabout and walk up Montague Street. Turn right on to Little Britain to the complex of **Barts ❿**. When you emerge on West Smithfield, turn left for the Henry VIII Gate and the historic part of the hospital. Founded in 1123, Barts is the oldest surviving hospital in England – though all that remains of its medieval fabric is on your left as you enter: the 15th-century chapel of St Bartholomew-the-Less. Walk through the first courtyard for the main square's North Wing, built by James Gibbs in the 1730s. It contains the Baroque **Great Hall** and the **Museum** (tel: 020-7601 8152; www.bartsandthelondon.nhs.uk; Tue–Fri 10am–4pm; free), which offers a history of the hospital as well as access to two spectacular murals (1736–7) by William Hogarth, who used real patients as some of his models.

SMITHFIELD MARKET

On the other side of West Smithfield is **Smithfield Market ⓫**, where livestock and meat have been traded since the 10th century. At various times the site has also been used for jousting, public executions (notably William Wallace's in 1305), the selling of wives and for Bartholomew Fair, which, from 1133 to 1855, drew crowds to its cloth market and pleasure fair. Today, the place is occupied by Sir Horace Jones's market buildings, built from 1866 above railway lines linking farmers and butchers across the country. The pubs around the market open famously early. People tipping out of the area's nightclubs can mingle with market workers over fried breakfasts and pints at 7am. If you want to be fed and watered, consider **Comptoir Gascon** or **Vinoteca**, see ⑪③ and ⑪④, on the far side of the market.

St Bartholomew-the-Great
As you come out of Little Britain on to West Smithfield, note this former monastic church (tel: 020-7606 5171; charge), with the finest Norman interior in London.

Food and Drink

③ COMPTOIR GASCON
61–3 Charterhouse Street; tel: 020-7608 0851; www.comptoirgascon.com; Tue–Sat L and D; ££–£££
An informal, tapas/bistro-style version of Club Gascon, on West Smithfield. Southern French dishes are cooked at both places.

④ VINOTECA
7 St John Street; tel: 020-7253 8786; www.vinoteca.co.uk; Mon–Sat L and D; ££–£££
Tasty modern European food, together with wines by the glass from a 200-strong list (also retailed from the shop). Recommended.

The Barbican

To the northeast of the Museum of London is the Barbican, a complex comprising 2,000 flats (in London's tallest residential towers) as well as a theatre, concert hall, cinema, art gallery, library, school, YMCA, fire station and even an ornamental lake. It was built by architects Chamberlin, Powell and Bon between 1965 and 1976 on a 35-acre (14-hectare) site that had been bombed in World War II. Despite numerous design problems – wind moans through the walkways, it is easy to get lost, the concrete was the wrong type and requires constant maintenance – it is still Britain's finest example of concrete Brutalist architecture, unrivalled for its scale, cohesion and attention to detail (from the specially designed carpets to the fitted kitchens).

THE SOUTH BANK

A riverside walk along the south bank of the Thames takes in some of the city's most important cultural institutions, as well as Shakespeare's London and the increasingly fashionable area around Borough Market.

Imperial War Museum

An optional detour from this route is to the Imperial War Museum (Lambeth Road; tel: 020-7416 5320; daily 10am–6pm; free), housed in a former hospital for the insane – an ironic choice for a museum that chronicles the horrors of modern war.

> **DISTANCE** 2 miles (3.5km)
> **TIME** Half to a full day
> **START** County Hall
> **END** London Bridge
> **GETTING AROUND**
> Allow a good half day (excluding museum/gallery visits). Do the walk on Friday or Saturday to see Borough Market in full swing.

The nearest tube station to the starting point is Waterloo. From here, leave by the overhead walkway signposted 'Southbank Centre', and as you descend the steps, you cannot miss the big wheel of the London Eye in front of you.

COUNTY HALL

Start at **County Hall ❶**, on your left as you reach the Eye. This huge Edwardian building was the seat of the Greater London Council until it was controversially disbanded by Margaret Thatcher in 1986. Now privately owned it contains two hotels, an aquarium, an art gallery, games arcade and several restaurants. **Namco Station** (tel: 020-7967 1067; www.namco station.co.uk; 10am–midnight; charge),

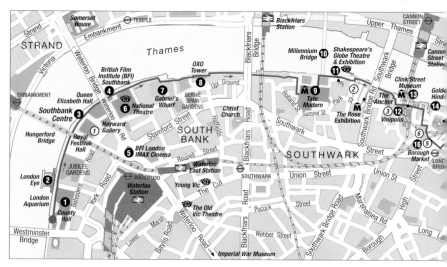

has bumper cars, video games and a bowling alley. Close by is the entrance to the **London Aquarium** (tel: 020-7967 8000; www.londonaquarium. co.uk; Mon–Thur 10am–6pm, Fri–Sun 10am–7pm; charge). Some 350 species are represented, but the highlight is the sharks. There is also a pool where you can touch some of the inhabitants. Feeding time for rainforest species, including piranhas, is Mon, Wed and Fri 1pm; for sharks, Tue, Thur and Sat 2.30pm.

LONDON EYE

Next stop is the **London Eye ❷** (tel: 0870-990 8883; www.londoneye.com; daily Apr–Aug 10am–9pm, Sept–Mar 10am–8.30pm; charge), the world's largest observation wheel, designed by husband-and-wife architects David Marks and Julia Barfield.

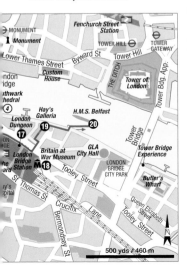

The 32 enclosed capsules take 30 minutes to make a full rotation, which is slow enough to let passengers step in and out of the capsules while the wheel is moving. On a clear day, you can see for 25 miles (40km). Book ahead if you want to ride at busy periods, and do check the weather forecast first.

SOUTHBANK CENTRE

Now continue along the riverside walk to the concrete bulk of the **Southbank Centre ❸** (contact for all venues unless otherwise indicated: tel: 020-7960 4200; www. southbankcentre. org.uk). The largest arts complex in Europe, it regularly puts on free entertainment, from lunch-time gigs and 'Commuter Jazz' (Fri 5.45–7pm) to talks on poetry and art. It is fronted by a row of restaurants (including Giraffe – a good choice if you have children), and a bookshop.

Music Venues

The **Royal Festival Hall** is a legacy of the 1951 Festival of Britain, intended to improve Londoners' morale after the austerity of the post-war years. In 2007, a major renovation of the hall was completed, giving it improved acoustics, better foyer facilities and two new restaurants: Skylon, with views of the river, and, around the back, the ground-floor **Canteen**, see ⓨⓘ *(p.64)*.

Next door are the 917-seat **Queen Elizabeth Hall** for music, dance and public lectures, and the 372-seat **Purcell Room**, for recitals of classical chamber music and world music.

Above from far left: the London Eye; Shakespeare's Globe; London Aquarium; crossing the Millennium Bridge from Tate Modern to St Paul's Cathedral.

Above: South Bank attractions: BFI's Imax cinema; The Clink.

London Eye Statistics
At 450ft (135m), the London Eye is the fourth tallest structure in London. The hub and spindle weigh 330 tonnes, more than 40 double-decker buses. On average, 10,000 people take a 'flight' on it every day.

Above from left: browsing the book-stalls in front of BFI Southbank; the Royal Festival Hall.

Iconic Design
As you pass the Hayward Gallery, look out for the neon tower on its roof. Commissioned in 1970 from Philip Vaughan and Roger Dainton for a Kinetics exhibition, this garish London landmark is composed of yellow, magenta, red, green and blue neon strips, which are controlled by changes in the direction and velocity of the wind.

Annual Frost Fair
On the third weekend in December, Bankside holds a fair (with an ice slide, stalls, and free events at the Globe), inspired by the Frost Fairs held whenever the Thames froze over in centuries

Hayward Gallery

Adjacent, on the upper level of the South Bank Centre complex, is the **Hayward Gallery** (Sun–Thur 10am–6pm, Fri–Sat 10am–10pm; www. hayward.org.uk; charge), one of London's most important venues for contemporary art exhibitions.

BFI Southbank

Next to the Hayward is Britain's leading arthouse cinema, **BFI Southbank ❹** (tel: 020-7928 3232; www.bfi.org.uk). With three auditoria and an intimate studio cinema, it holds more than 2,400 screenings and events every year, from talks by film stars to silent movies with live accompaniment. The cinema also houses a research area, a shop, and an excellent 'Mediathèque', where visitors can browse the British Film Institute's archive for free (call ahead

---

Food and Drink 🍴

①　CANTEEN
Royal Festival Hall; tel: 0845-686 1122; www.canteen.co.uk; daily B, L and D; ££
Situated at the back of the Festival Hall, it serves good-quality modern British food in a sleek white interior as well as on the heated terrace outside.

②　TAS PIDE
20–2 New Globe Walk; tel: 020-7633 9777; www.tasrestaurant.com; daily L and D; ££
A wide choice of *meze*, as well as *pide* (Turkish pizza), grilled sardines and lamb kofta. Branches also in Borough High Street (tel: 020-7403 7200), near London Bridge, and The Cut (tel: 020-7926 2111), near Waterloo.

---

to reserve). For a drink before a screening, try the ever-popular Film Café in front of the building, with tables and benches sheltering under Waterloo Bridge, or, for more plush surroundings, visit the upstairs **Benugo Bar & Kitchen**.

The **BFI** also runs **London Imax ❺** (tel: 0870-787 2525), a 5-minute walk away in the centre of the roundabout at the southern end of Waterloo Bridge. This cylindrical, glass building houses Britain's largest cinema screen, together with steeply raked seating.

NATIONAL THEATRE

Just to the east of the Southbank complex is the **National Theatre ❻** (020-7452 3400; www.nationaltheatre. org.uk). Built to designs by Sir Denys Lasdun and opened in 1976, this concrete behemoth houses three theatres: the 1,200-seat Olivier, the 900-seat Lyttelton and the Cottesloe (shortly to be refurbished and renamed the Dorfman, after a major sponsor), a more intimate space with galleries on three sides. For a peek behind the scenes, book a one-hour backstage tour (see website for times; charge).

OXO TOWER

After the theatres, you pass **Gabriel's Wharf ❼**, with restaurants and gift shops, and, close by, the Art Deco **OXO Tower ❽**. Architect Albert Moore had grand ideas for this project: as well as erecting what was to become London's second highest commercial

building, he wanted to use electric lights to spell out the product's name. When planning permission was refused because of an advertising ban, Moore came up with the idea of using three letters – O, X and O – as windows looking out north, south, east and west. Inside the tower are several smart restaurants; it's a glamorous, and expensive, spot for cocktails with stunning river views.

TATE MODERN

To the east of Blackfriars Bridge lies the former colossal Bankside Power Station, which is now **Tate Modern** ⑨, home to the Tate's international contemporary art collection (covered in detail in the Tate to Tate tour, *see p.68*).

In front of Tate Modern is the graceful **Millennium Bridge** ⑩, a pedestrian link to St Paul's Cathedral (*see p.59*). Unveiled in 2000, it was the first new river crossing over the Thames in central London since Tower Bridge in 1894. However, on its opening day, crowds on the bridge caused it to sway alarmingly, and it had to close for structural amendments by its architect, Norman (now Lord) Foster. By 2002, the wobble was fixed, and it reopened.

SHAKESPEARE'S GLOBE

Heading a little further east, you reach Bankside, one of the South Bank's most historic areas. The district grew up in competition with the City opposite, but by the 16th century had become a den of vice, famous for

brothels, bear- and bull-baiting pits, prize-fights and the first playhouses, including the Globe.

A replica of the original (1599) open-air Globe Theatre, called **Shakespeare's Globe** ⑪, opened here in 1996 after years of fund-raising. The thatched roof was the first permitted in London since the Great Fire of 1666. **Shakespeare's Globe Exhibition** (tel: 020-7902 1500; www.shakespeares globe.org; May–Sept daily 9am–noon, Oct–Apr daily 10am–5pm; charge), to the right of the theatre, fills in the background on the area's historic past. Just opposite is **Tas Pide**, see ⑪②, a good place for a spot of lunch.

Cheap Seats

The National Theatre's director, Nicholas Hytner, has had some success in broadening the theatre's appeal by offering some cheaper seats (from £12, including some seats in the stalls) for productions sponsored by Travelex. Book as far ahead as possible.

Below: giant furniture promoting the National Theatre's free 'Watch This Space' festival.

Above from left:
nature's bounty at
Borough Market;
William Shakespeare;
sign at Gabriel's
Wharf; remnant of
Winchester Palace on
Clink Street.

Below:
warehouses below
the OXO Tower.

BANK END AND CLINK STREET

At Bank End is the Anchor pub, where little has changed in 200 years. Across the street, in the vaults under the railway viaduct, is **Vinopolis** ⑫ (tel: 0207-940 3000; www.vinopolis.co.uk; wine tasting tours Thur–Fri 2–10pm, Sat noon–10pm, Sun noon–6pm; charge), and has a huge wine shop and smart restaurant, see ⑪③.

The Clink

On **Clink Street** are the fragments of the Bishop of Winchester's 13th-century residence, from which the bishops operated a prison. The phrase 'in the clink', a euphemism for being in jail, is thought to stem from the sound made by clanking chains. The **Clink Street Museum** ⑬ (tel: 0207-403 0900; www.clink.co.uk; July–Sept daily 10am–9pm, Oct–June Mon–Fri 10am–6pm, Sat–Sun 10am–7.30pm; charge) recalls the area's gruesome past.

The Golden Hinde

At the far end of Clink Street is St Mary Overy Dock, where parishioners were once able to land goods free of toll and have their wives put in the ducking stool. A gleaming replica of Sir Francis Drake's diminutive ship the **Golden Hinde** ⑭ (tel: 0207-403 0123; www.goldenhinde.co.uk; daily 10am–5.30pm; charge) now sits in the dock.

SOUTHWARK CATHEDRAL

Follow the road round to the right then bear left to **Southwark Cathedral** ⑮ (tel: 020-7367 6700; www.southwark.anglican.org; daily 8am–6pm; free). Shakespeare was a parishioner here, and a memorial in the south aisle shows him reclining in front of a frieze showing Bankside during the 16th century. John Harvard, who gave his name to the American university, was baptised here, and is commemorated in the Harvard Chapel. Organ recitals are held in the cathedral on Monday at 1pm and classical concerts on Tuesday at 3.15pm (both free). The refectory, see ⑪④, is a cosy place for refreshment.

BOROUGH MARKET

In the shelter of the cathedral is **Borough Market** ⑯, a food market dating back to the 13th century. On Thursday, Friday and Saturday the market sells gourmet and organic products. As well as fruit, vegetables, bread and cheese, you will find stalls specialising in game, fish, cakes, preserves, ecologically sound produce,

wines and beers, with lots of opportunities to sample the produce. Many stalls do takeaway food, from venison burgers to scallops pan-fried while you wait. **Tapas Brindisa**, see ⑪⑤ and **Roast**, see ⑪⑥ are two excellent options for lunch.

TOWARDS TOWER BRIDGE

To the east of the market is London Bridge Station and the newly built **Shard**, Europe's tallest building. You can finish the tour here, but if you still have some energy, continue east on Tooley Street, just beyond the station to the **London Dungeon** ⑰ (tel: 020-7403 7221; www.thedungeons.com; daily July–Aug 9.30am–6.30pm, Sept–June 10am–5.30pm; charge). Lasting about 1½ hours, a tour led by actors features ghoulish exhibits on the Black Death, the Great Fire of 1666 and Jack the Ripper's exploits, as well as several ghost-train-style rides.

It is fun for children who like the macabre, but the visit is spent in darkened corridors, so it is not recommended for those under eight. Note that queues can be long and tickets are expensive.

Next door is the **Britain at War Experience** ⑱ (tel: 020-7403 3171; www.britainatwar.co.uk; daily 10am–5pm; charge), which recreates the atmosphere of the Blitz. Across the road is an old wharf, now filled in and renamed **Hay's Galleria** ⑲, a smart atrium of shops and restaurants.

Continuing through to the riverside, you cannot miss the World War II cruiser HMS *Belfast* ⑳ (tel: 020-7940

6300; www.iwm.org.uk; tours daily 10am–6pm; charge).

If you continue east you reach Tower Bridge, where you could cross the bridge to link up with tour 9 *(see p.57)*. Alternatively, return to London Bridge for the tube or mainline train.

Food and Drink 🍴

③ VINOPOLIS
1 Bank End; tel: 020-7940 8333; www.cantinavinopolis.co.uk; L Thur–Sat, D Mon–Sat; ££
Cavernous wine vaults accommodate a restaurant serving good modern British food and, not surprisingly, an exceptional wine list.

④ SOUTHWARK CATHEDRAL REFECTORY
London Bridge; tel: 020-7407 5740; www.southwark.anglican.org; daily B, L and AT; £–££
The restaurant at the back of the cathedral offers wholesome soups and main dishes at reasonable prices. Outside tables on the terrace in summer.

⑤ TAPAS BRINDISA
18–20 Southwark Street; tel: 020-7357 8880; www.brindisa.com; Fri–Sat B, L, D, Sun–Thur L and D; £££
Usually packed thanks to its authentic tapas and a buzzing ambience. The only downside is that they do not take reservations.

⑥ ROAST
Floral Hall, Stoney Street; tel: 020-7940 1300; www.roast-restaurant.com; Mon–Sat B, L, D, Sun D; £££/££££; set meal (Mon–Fri L) ££
Delicious British food includes succulent organic Banham chicken and sturdy game pies. Breakfasts are scrumptious and reasonably priced.

Globe Productions
The season of this open-air theatre *(see p.65)* runs from May to early October. The theatre can accommodate around 1,500 people – 600 standing (and liable to get wet if it rains) and the rest seated. The wooden benches feel rather hard by Act III, but you can bring or rent cushions. If you have a bargain 'groundling' ticket, bring waterproofs, in case of downpours; note that the use of umbrellas is not allowed in the auditorium during performances. If you cannot make it to a show, consider going on one of the theatre tours instead.

Did You Know?
Bankside Power Station – now Tate Modern – opened in 1963 but generated electricity for little more than 30 years before being declared redundant.

11

TATE TO TATE

Visit Tate Modern, one of London's top tourist attractions, and one of the world's most innovative modern art museums, then speed up the river by catamaran to Tate Britain for a survey of British art through the centuries.

DISTANCE 2¼ miles (3.5km) not including distance in galleries
TIME A full day
START Tate Modern, Southwark
END Tate Britain, Pimlico
POINTS TO NOTE
If you book your boat trip on arrival at Tate Modern, you can enjoy the morning at Bankside, take the boat to Pimlico, have lunch, then spend the afternoon at Tate Britain. Alternatively, combine this tour with walk 10, covering the South Bank.

Peregrine Falcons
During recent summers, when not chasing their lunch through the air, peregrine falcons have roosted on the 325ft (99m) high chimney of Tate Modern. Bird conservationists set up their telescopes below, so that members of the public can get a good view.

There are now two Tate galleries in London, and two outside, in Liverpool and St Ives. The original foundation for the gallery was laid by Henry Tate (who made a fortune by inventing the sugar lump); it opened in 1897 as a department of the National Gallery. The collection now also encompasses the national holdings of international modern and contemporary art.

TATE MODERN

The route begins on the south bank of the river at **Tate Modern ❶** (tel: 020-7887 8888; www.tate.org.uk; Sun–Thur 10am–6pm, Fri–Sat 10am–10pm; free). The nearest tube stations are London Bridge or Southwark (south of the river) and Blackfriars (to the north), all about 10 minutes' walk away. The lamp-posts between Southwark tube station and the gallery are painted orange to show visitors the way.

The Building

In 1998, the Tate made the bold decision to purchase the disused Bankside Power Station, and Swiss architects Herzog & de Meuron won the competition to transform it into an art gallery. The industrial character of Sir Giles Gilbert Scott's original brick structure (built in two stages between 1947 and

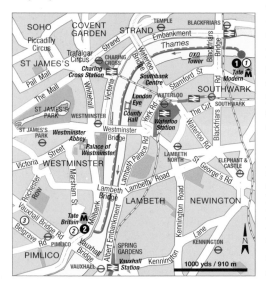

1963) was retained. They saved the vast Turbine Hall for housing large-scale art installations, reopened the block's monumental windows and fitted a light at the top of the huge central chimney.

The Collection

The permanent collection at Tate Modern is displayed in four suites, over two floors (levels 3 and 5), and focuses on definitive moments in 20th-century art history: Surrealism, Minimalism, post-war Abstraction, and the three linked movements of Cubism, Futurism and Vorticism. The galleries on level 4 stage temporary exhibitions, often of international importance. There is also a restaurant on level 7, see 🍴①.

Level 3

On level 3 is 'Material Gestures', using post-war abstract European and American painting and sculpture as a focal point, with precursors and successors traced alongside. The works of Barnett Newman and Anish Kapoor are shown together, as are paintings by Claude Monet and Mark Rothko. Abstract Expressionism is displayed in the context of earlier figurative expressionism. Worth a quiet moment is the room devoted to Rothko's sombre *Seagram Murals* (1958–9), commissioned for a restaurant in the Seagram Building on Park Avenue, New York. It is not hard to see why Rothko decided they would sit better in a less commercial setting.

Next, 'Poetry and Dream' focuses on Surrealism, embracing the diverse range of techniques and styles of Miró, Ernst, Dalí, Magritte, Klee and Man Ray. Their influence is then pursued to Picasso and Pollock, Francis Bacon and Joseph Beuys, Cindy Sherman and Gillian Wearing, as well as to cinema, periodicals, and performance art.

Level 5

Level 5 starts with 'Energy and Process', which looks at explorations of transformation and natural forces through the use of industrial and organic materials, the everyday and the finely crafted, the photographic and the painterly. Much space is given to the Italian Arte Povera movement, noted for its scepticism about capitalism and consumerism; and works by Donald Judd, Carl Andre and Richard Long, which examine material and form, and blur distinctions between artwork and context.

Finally comes 'States of Flux', devoted to Cubism, Futurism and Vorticism. Alongside classic statements of these approaches – by Braque, Picasso, Boccioni and Wyndham Lewis – their influence is shown cropping up in various quarters, from the graphic design of Stalinist Russia to the collages of Pop Art.

Food and Drink 🍴

① TATE MODERN RESTAURANT
Level 7, Tate Modern, Bankside; tel: 020-7401 5018; www.tate.org.uk; Sun–Thur L, Fri–Sat L and D; £££
Wonderful views of London, pleasant hubbub and a style-conscious crowd. Fresh Cornish fish is a speciality. The Level 2 Café, by the ground-floor bookshop, is an alternative, and cheaper, lunch option.

Above from far left: artist Damien Hirst and Tate Director Nicholas Serota with Hirst's *Mother and Child Divided 2007* in 'Turner Prize: A Retrospective' at Tate Britain; view from Tate Modern over the Thames and the Millennium Bridge to St Paul's; studying the artworks at Tate Modern; the Turbine Hall.

The Turbine Hall
This vast hall is five storeys tall, with 37,000 sq ft (3,400 sq m) of floor space, and is used for specially commissioned work by contemporary artists. In 2003, Olafur Eliasson devised *The Weather Project*, with a mirror sky, sun and mist, while in 2007, Doris Salcedo created *Shibboleth*, consisting of a crack running through the concrete floor. In 2010, Ai Weiwei covered the floor with 100 million hand-painted porcelain sunflower seeds.

Above from left:
John Everett Millais's
Ophelia (1851–2),
a highlight of Tate
Britain's permanent
collection; sign for the
river boat.

Turner Prize
The country's most
prestigious and
controversial annual art
prize is usually hosted
at Tate Britain. Many
criticise the judges'
predilection for
conceptual artists,
such as Tracey Emin,
who in 1999
submitted her own
double bed or Richard
Deacon, whose *For
Those Who Have Eyes*
(1983) is shown
above. In 2002, culture
minister Kim Howells
left feedback at the
exhibition of shortlisted
artists: 'if this is the
best British artists can
produce then British
art is lost,' and
followed this up with a
choice expletive while
decrying conceptual
artists' 'lack of
conviction'. Others,
however, credit the
prize with raising the
profile of British art.

TATE BOAT

The **Tate Boat** runs every forty minutes during gallery opening hours, shuttling back and forth between Tate Britain and Tate Modern, and stopping off at the London Eye along the way.

Tickets are available from Tate Modern and Tate Britain, as well as online and by calling 020-7887 8888, or, subject to availability, on the boat itself.

Embarking from the small pier in front of Tate Modern, you are taken in the 220-seat catamaran (with exterior and interior designs by artist Damien Hirst) to Millbank pier in front of Tate Britain. The pier was designed by architects David Marks and Julia Barfield, who were also responsible for the London Eye. It features a lighting installation by

artist Angela Bulloch, who was shortlisted for the 1997 Turner Prize. Fluorescent tubing embedded into the floor of the pontoon is computer programmed to provide changing lighting effects at night.

TATE BRITAIN

Tate Britain ❷ (Millbank; tel: 020-7887 8000; www.tate.org.uk; daily 10am–6pm, until 10pm Fri; free) in Pimlico is the original Tate Gallery and home to the national collection of British art from 1500 to the present day. Opened in 1897, it was designed by Sydney Smith in classical style, and built on the site of a prison.

The permanent collection is almost entirely contained on one floor (level 2) and is organised roughly chronologically. As you enter the building through the front porticoed entrance on Millbank, you go through a succession of grand halls with galleries off to the left and right.

Art from 1350 to 1800
Walking beyond the octagon to the hall at the back you will find rooms displaying English alabaster sculptures from *c*.1350–1450 and Tudor and Stuart portraits, including Nicholas Hilliard's painting (*c*.1575) of Queen Elizabeth I in one of her bejewelled dresses.

Subsequent rooms take you through the 17th and 18th centuries, with glamorous portraits by Van Dyck, social satire by Hogarth, and aristocratic portraits and allegorical scenes

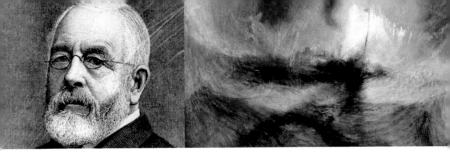

in the Grand Manner by painters including Gainsborough, Reynolds, and one of the few women artists of the time, Angelica Kauffman.

Romanticism and Victorian Art

Many of the galleries on the east side of the gallery are devoted to the transition from a classicising to romantic aesthetic. This is most explicit in the depiction of the natural world. The landscape painting of John Constable is well represented here, while the seascapes of J.M.W. Turner have their own dedicated wing of the museum, the Clore Gallery *(see box, below)*.

The following rooms are rich in Victorian genre painting, with its narrative content and obsessive period detail. Also here are the Pre-Raphaelites who created sharply realistic paintings in pure, brilliant colours. Millais's romantic *Ophelia* (1851–2) is one of the gallery's most popular pictures.

Modern Art

On the west side of the gallery, towards the front of the building, are rooms devoted to 20th-century British art. As well as discernible movements such as Vorticism and Pop Art, and groups such as those from Camden Town and St Ives, there are also modern masters who do not fit so easily into categories: Stanley Spencer, Francis Bacon and Lucian Freud among them.

When you have finished your survey of British art, retire to the restaurant downstairs ⑪②, or else head for the dependable **Grumbles**, see ⑪③, just off Belgrave Road to the north of Pimlico tube station.

Late at the Tate
Every Friday Tate Britain stays open until 10pm, and special exhibition entry is half-price. There is also an excellent programme of performances, music, talks and films, though these tend to be very popular, so arrive early to queue for the free tickets.

Turner Bequest

On his death in 1851, London-born Joseph Mallord William Turner (1775–1851) left a large sum of money and his collection of 20,000 paintings and drawings to the British nation, expressing the wish that a special gallery be built to house them all together. It took until 1987 for this to happen, when the Clore Gallery, designed by British architect James Stirling, was opened beside Tate Britain. Even now, however, some of his paintings are scattered across other collections, contrary to his wishes. Masterpieces on display include *Peace – Burial at Sea*, showing the artist's mastery in depicting light as affected by objects, rather than the other way round, and *Snow Storm: Steam-Boat off a Harbour's Mouth*, suggestive of Turner's fascination with the elemental forces of nature. In order to paint the sensational effect achieved in the latter, Turner tells us in his subtitle that 'The Author was in this Storm on the Night the *Ariel* left Harwich', lashed, at his own request, to the ship's mast.

HYDE PARK

On May Day 1660, Samuel Pepys wrote in his diary, 'It being a very pleasant day I wished myself in Hyde Park.' Three and a half centuries later, in the heart of a much-changed London, people still feel exactly the same way.

Speakers' Corner
People have been congregating in the northeast corner of the park to air their views since the 18th century. Before that, it was the location of the Tyburn hanging tree, where executions had taken place since the 12th century. The right of public assembly here was formalised in law in 1872 following the Reform League's large rallies in 1866 and 1867 in support of the right of working-class men to vote. Famous speakers here have included Karl Marx, Friedrich Engels, Vladimir Lenin, William Morris, George Orwell and the Pankhursts. Over a million people, the largest turn-out in its history, protested here in 2003 against the Iraq War.

Upside-Down Tree
Near the rose gardens is the Weeping Beech, *Fagus sylvatica pendula*, cherished as 'the upside-down tree'.

DISTANCE 2¾ miles (4.5km)
TIME Half a day
START Apsley House
END Queensway tube
POINTS TO NOTE

People with restricted mobility can book an electric buggy, driven by a volunteer (tel: 07767-498096; May–Oct Tue–Fri 10am–5pm).

Hyde Park was first opened to the public in 1637 by Charles I. It had previously been a deer park used by Henry VIII for hunting and, before that, a manor owned by Westminster Abbey since before the Norman Conquest.

The adjacent Kensington Gardens were sectioned off as the grounds of Kensington Palace in 1689, when William III moved here from Whitehall Palace. Today, all 625 acres (253 hectares) of the park are once again open to the public.

Food and Drink 🍴
① THE DELL CAFÉ
South side of the Serpentine; tel: 020-7706 7098; daily summer 9am–8pm, winter 9am–4pm; £–££
A pavilion with a terrace overlooking the Serpentine. Serves simple meals and snacks.

APSLEY HOUSE

The route begins at **Apsley House ❶** (tel: 020-7499 5676; www.english-heritage.org.uk; Apr–Oct Wed–Sun 11am–5pm, Nov–Mar Sat–Sun 10am–4pm; charge), near Exit 1 of Hyde Park Corner tube station. Once known as No. 1 London, since it was the first house encountered after passing the tollgates of Knightsbridge, this was where the Duke of Wellington lived from 1817 until his death in 1852. Part of the house is still home to his descendants today.

The house was designed by the architect Robert Adam, and was built between 1771 and 1778. On its passing to the Duke of Wellington, the house had its original brick exterior faced with stone, and the portico and columns were added. Inside, however, much of the original Adam design survives, including the staircase, drawing room and portico room.

Following the Duke's victory at Waterloo, gratitude was heaped upon him in the form of plate and porcelain, paintings, sculpture and chandeliers. The art collection includes works by Goya, Rubens, Correggio and Brueghel. One gift he should perhaps have refused is an 11ft (3.4m) high nude statue of Napoleon that dominates the stairwell.

HYDE PARK

Enter **Hyde Park** ❷ (tel: 020-7298 2100; www.royalparks.org.uk; daily 5am–midnight; free) via the **Triumphal Screen** to the left of Apsley House. This monumental entrance was commissioned from Decimus Burton by King George IV in the 1820s along with the Wellington Arch, which was later moved to the middle of the roundabout.

If you are fortunate to be here in mid-morning, you might wait at this point to see the Household Cavalry who emerge from their barracks at 10.30am every morning (9.30am on Sunday) on South Carriage Drive and ride across the park to Horse Guards Parade for the changing of the guard. The other road (unmetalled) running east–west and converging on Hyde Park Corner is **Rotten Row** – a corruption of Route du Roi – the king's route from Kensington Palace to Westminster. It was the first road in England to be lit at night – by 300 oil lamps. The Crystal Palace, the spectacular iron-and-glass showcase of the 1851 Great Exhibition, once stood between the two roads. (It was later moved to Sydenham Hill, in southeast London, but burnt down in 1936.)

The Serpentine

Now take the Serpentine Road northwest, past the bandstand on your right, and the rose gardens on your left, to the northern bank of the **Serpentine** ❸. This lake was created by Queen Caroline in 1730 by damming the river Westbourne. It achieved notoriety in December 1816 when the pregnant wife of the poet Shelley committed suicide by plunging into the icy waters; Shelley married Mary Wollstonecraft Godwin two weeks later. Today, the lake has its own swimming club and is the scene of a famous Christmas Day 100-yard race (tel: 020 7706 3422; www.serpentine lido.com).

Above from far left: leafy Hyde Park; the Serpentine running through it.

Below: commemorative wreaths; Household Cavalry in Hyde Park.

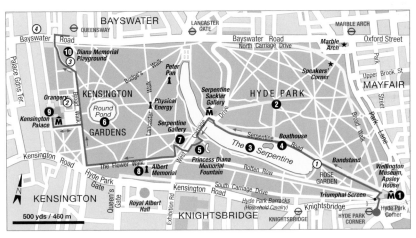

Skating

Each December Hyde Park hosts an ice-skating rink. In the summer, rollerbladers meet en masse at the bandstand (every Wed 7.30pm).

Queen's Temple

Walk northwest from the Serpentine Gallery to find Queen Caroline's Temple on your right (built 1734–5 by William Kent). Further up is a statue, *Physical Energy* by G.F. Watts (1907).

On your left as you come to the lake is the **Dell Café**, see ①① *(p.72)* and further round is the **Boathouse ④**, where you can hire rowing boats and pedalos (Mar–Oct), or take a trip on the solar-powered ferry.

A little further on, West Carriage Drive marks the boundary between Hyde Park and Kensington Gardens. Turn left, and just before the bridge is the **Powder Magazine**. This was originally used for storing gunpowder, but from 2012 it becomes an annexe of the Serpentine Gallery *(see right)*.

To the left of the road on the other side of the bridge is the **Princess Diana Memorial Fountain ⑤**, designed by American architect Kathryn Gustafson. This innovative fountain has been dogged by controversy since opening in 2004, owing to the initial cost (£3.6m), and the heavy burdens of ongoing maintenance and supervision. However, it's a popular spot, and children love paddling in its shallow waters.

KENSINGTON GARDENS

Cross over West Carriage Drive and you enter **Kensington Gardens ⑥** (tel: 020-7298 2141; www.royalparks.org.uk; daily 6am–dusk; free). You might have been denied the pleasure of access had Queen Caroline (wife of George II) had her way. On enquiring of Prime Minister Walpole what the cost might be of reclaiming the, by then, public gardens for her private use, she received the reply, 'Only a Crown, Madam'.

Serpentine Gallery

Follow the path off the road for the **Serpentine Gallery ⑦** (tel: 020-7402 6075; www.serpentinegallery.org; daily 10am–6pm; free). This classical-style 1934 tea pavilion puts on major exhibitions of modern and contemporary art. Every spring, a leading architect (Daniel Libeskind, Rem Koolhaas, *et al*), is commissioned to build a temporary pavilion (June–Sept) alongside it.

Albert Memorial

Now follow the signposts along the southwesterly path for the **Albert Memorial ⑧**, commissioned by Queen Victoria in memory of her beloved husband, Prince Albert, who died of typhoid in 1861. This Gothic-revival monument was designed by Sir George Gilbert Scott and unveiled in 1872. It centres around a gilded Albert holding a catalogue of the Great Exhibition of 1851. He is surrounded by massive representations of the continents and sits enshrined in a white marble frieze depicting 187 poets and painters. The

---

Food and Drink 🍴

② THE ORANGERY
Kensington Gardens; tel: 020-7166 6112; daily B, L and AT 10am–6pm, till 5pm in winter; £–££
Light lunches and afternoon tea. Outside seating in summer.

③ BROADWALK CAFÉ
Kensington Gardens; tel: 020-7034 0722; daily summer B, L and D, 8am–8pm, winter B and L 10am–4pm; £
Ideal for children. Serves salads, pizzas, fruit, yoghurts, ice creams.

④ CAFÉ DIANA
5 Wellington Terrace, Bayswater Road; tel: 020-7792 9606; daily B, L and early D 10am–6pm; £–££
The walls are plastered with photos of the princess. Serves a wide variety of snacks as well as all-day breakfasts and some Middle Eastern dishes.

180ft (55m) spire is inlaid with semi-precious stones.

Across the road to the south is the **Royal Albert Hall** (tel: 020-7589 3203; www.royalalberthall.com), opened in 1871, and now the venue for concerts, including the Proms every summer.

Kensington Palace

Next, to reach **Kensington Palace** ❾ (tel: 020-7937 9561; www.hrp.org.uk; daily Mar–Oct 10am–6pm, Nov–Feb 10am–5pm; charge), continue west, and take a path off to your right in a northwesterly direction. The house came into royal hands in 1689, when William III bought it in the hope that the country air would alleviate his asthma. Additions were made at this time by Sir Christopher Wren, and later by William Kent for George I. Since then it has been inhabited by various members of the Royal Family, most notably Princess Diana, who lived here until her death in 1997; and currently by Prince William and the Duchess of Cambridge.

Highlights inside include the Ceremonial Dress Collection, which has 14 dresses worn by Princess Diana as well as lavish costumes worn for state occasions. Also impressive is the King's Staircase, with wall paintings of George I's court by William Kent: look out for the king's Polish page Ulric, the Turkish servants Mahomet and Mustapha, Peter 'the wild boy' – a feral child found in the woods in Germany – and a portrait of the artist himself, with his mistress at his shoulder, looking down from the ceiling.

The Palace Gardens

Outside again, just to the east, near the path by which you entered, is the sunken Dutch garden, and on the other side of the path, a statue of Queen Victoria sculpted by her daughter, Princess Louise, to celebrate 50 years of her mother's reign.

To the north is Hawksmoor's **Orangery**, where Queen Anne liked to take tea, and you can too, see 🍽②. Beyond that is the **Diana, Princess of Wales Memorial Playground** ❿, where children can make up for having been so well behaved in the tearoom. And when they are tired of clambering over the huge pirate ship at the playground's centre, there is another café for ice creams and cakes, see 🍽③.

Finally, in the northwest corner of the park, leave by the Orme Square Gate, which after 5pm (4pm in winter) is the only exit open. On Bayswater Road, turn right for Queensway tube or left for **Café Diana**, see 🍽④.

Horse Riding

The park is well adapted to horse riding, with its own specialist arena, or 'Manège', as well as two designated bridle paths. If you fancy following in the hoof steps of the Cavalry, contact Stanhorse Riding (Hyde Park and Kensington Stables, 63 Bathurst Mews, Lancaster Gate; tel: 020-7723 2813; www.hydepark stables.com).

Peter Pan

Walk north from the Serpentine Gallery and in a leafy glade by the Long Water is a statue of Peter Pan. It was here that the Llewelyn Davies children, who inspired the Peter Pan stories, were brought to play by the author J.M. Barrie (he had become co-guardian after their parents died). In one story, Peter Pan flies out of his nursery and lands beside the Long Water, on the spot where the statue now stands. The sculpture was made by Sir George Frampton and put up in the middle of the night of 1 May 1912 to surprise children playing in the park the next day.

SOUTH KENSINGTON AND KNIGHTSBRIDGE

Museums of decorative arts, natural history and science – the Victorians' rich legacy – are the improving highlights of this tour, after which you can make a less edifying, but equally enjoyable, visit to Harrods.

Crystal Palace
Joseph Paxton's design for a crystal palace was a late entry in the competition to find a suitable structure in which to house the Great Exhibition. Paxton was in fact not a professionally trained architect at all, but the former gardener to the Duke of Devonshire.

DISTANCE 1¼ miles (2km) not including distance covered in museums
TIME A full day
START South Kensington tube
END Knightsbridge
POINTS TO NOTE
All three museums are vast, and visiting all of them in one day would be exhausting; concentrate on one or two, according to interest. Entrance is, however, free, meaning that popping in to see one or two prize exhibits in each is perfectly feasible.

The year 1851 is remembered in Britain for the Great Exhibition, held in Hyde Park in a glass-and-metal palace designed by Joseph Paxton. Aspects of the far-flung Victorian Empire were brought under the curious gaze of a public whose interest in the sciences and the arts had seemingly never been greater. The idea for the exhibition came from Henry Cole (1808–82), chairman of the Society of Arts, and was taken up enthusiastically by the royal consort Prince Albert, who chaired the committee to see it through. Housed in a 'Crystal Palace' built in the park, the event attracted more than 6 million visitors. Afterwards, the building was moved to Sydenham, southeast London, and the exhibition's huge profits were used to purchase 87 acres (35 hectares) in South Kensington to build a more permanent home for the arts and sciences. This area is the focal point of this tour.

V&A

Start at **South Kensington tube station**, where a good place for lunch is **Daquise**, see ⑪①. When you are ready to head on to the museums, take the underpass in the tube station sign-

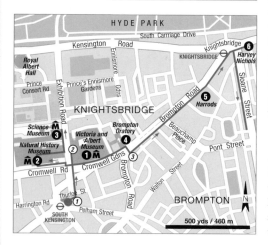

posted 'Museums', which brings you out on to Cromwell Road, beside the **Victoria and Albert Museum ❶** (tel: 020-7942 2000; www. vam.ac.uk; daily 10am–5.45pm, Fri until 10pm; free).

The Foyer

The museum is vast, with around 5 million objects in its collection, stored in about 8 miles (13km) of galleries. Start in the main foyer, where you can admire the Venetian-inspired 'chandelier' by American artist Dale Chihuly. The spectacular accretion of blue, green and yellow glass was erected in 1999 as a talking-point for the Victorian foyer, and was doubled in size in 2001 to a height of (33ft) 10m. It was assembled *in situ* by a team of technicians, each piece of glass slotted over an angled rod.

Lower Ground and Ground Floors

On the ground floor, the first galleries on either side of the entrance hall and gift shop display the Asian collections, with treasures from China, Japan, India and the Middle East. Highlights include spectacular rugs and carpets, and the extraordinary *Tipu's Tiger*, a carved automaton of an Indian tiger killing a British officer, made *c.*1790 for Sultan Tipu.

To the far left of the entrance (in room 48a) are the vast *Raphael Cartoons* (1515–16), on loan from the Queen. These drawings, depict scenes from the lives of St Peter and St Paul, and were commissioned by Pope Leo X as templates for a series of tapestries in the Sistine Chapel. Nearby, in room 40, is the revamped fashion gallery.

Flanking the great courtyard are the **Sculpture Courts**, which display masterpieces from around the world. To the rear of the courtyard, near the Ceramic Staircase (which symbolises the symbiotic relationship between art and science), are the three original refreshment rooms, where first-, second- and third-class menus were served prior to World War II. Allusions to food and drink are worked into the decoration. The room by Arts and Crafts pioneers William Morris, Philip Webb and Edward Burne-Jones is particularly fine.

Upper Floors

Upstairs, most galleries focus on materials or techniques, such as silver, ironwork (home to Sir George Gilbert Scott's intricate 1862 Hereford Screen), stained glass, ceramics (most of the top floor), textiles and jewellery. The **British Galleries**, charting British taste from 1500 to 1900, are in rooms 52–8.

Henry Cole Wing

The last remaining section is the Henry Cole Wing, spread over six floors and devoted mostly to changing

Above from far left: V&A entrance; Prince Albert; glass staircase and exhibit in the Cast Courts, V&A.

Below: 16th-century Iranian Ardabil carpet; Chihuly's 'chandelier' in the foyer.

Late Opening

Henry Cole began assembling the V&A collection the year after the Great Exhibition, but Queen Victoria did not lay the foundation stone of the current building until 1899, 38 years after Albert's death.

Food and Drink

① DAQUISE

20 Thurloe Street; tel: 020-7589 6117; www.gesslerlondon.com; daily 11.30am–11pm; Mon–Fri set lunch; ££

Reach this Polish restaurant by taking the right-hand exit out of South Kensington tube, and turning immediately right. Daquise is at the end of the row of shops. A loyal Polish and local clientele come here for the excellent authentic food at reasonable prices (especially for this up-market area). The decor, including the squishy banquettes, has not changed for decades.

Above from left: the Natural History Museum's main hall; escalator up to a globe – the entrance to the Earth Galleries.

Terrible Lizards
On the landing of the Natural History Museum, overlooking the main hall, is a statue of Richard Owen, the museum's first director. He was the first to recognise the existence of giant prehistoric land reptiles and called them dinosaurs ('terrible lizards').

Below: the Natural History Museum's Mammals section.

exhibitions of prints, drawings, paintings and photographs. Also here is the **Frank Lloyd Wright Room**, transplanted here from Pittsburgh, and the only example of the architect's work in Europe. End the tour here with a visit to the museum's café, see ⑪②.

NATURAL HISTORY MUSEUM

Across Exhibition Road is the neo-Gothic **Natural History Museum ❷** (tel: 020-7942 5000; www.nhm.ac.uk; daily 10am–5.50pm; free). The collection was originally a department of the British Museum, but by the middle of the 19th century it had expanded and outgrown the available space, and in 1881 the present museum opened; it

now houses around 75 million plants, animals, fossils, rocks and minerals.

Life Galleries

The first half of the museum is classed as the 'Life Galleries', although ironically its chief attractions – the dinosaurs – are well and truly dead. Just past the information desks, in the middle of the Central Hall, is the cast of a diplodocus unearthed in Wyoming in 1899. At 85ft (26m), it is the longest complete dinosaur skeleton ever discovered.

The **Dinosaur Gallery** is one of the busiest sections of the museum, and many visitors make a bee-line for the robotic dinosaurs at the far end. The full-scale animatronic **T-Rex** on long-term loan from Japan is responsive to human movement; the roaring, life-like model twists and turns, delighting most children (and frightening some).

Human Biology examines the workings behind the human body, from hormones to genes, and is packed with interactive exhibits that will test your memory or trick your senses with optical illusions.

The spectacular suspension of a life-sized blue whale model is the highlight of the **Mammals** section. As well as displaying an astonishing array of taxidermy, these galleries contain sobering statistics on the rate at which species are becoming extinct.

The gallery of **Fish, Amphibians and Reptiles** includes some fascinating species, such as the fish that live between between the sea's twilight zone at 1,300ft (400m) and total darkness at 3,300ft (1,000m). Next door

is the serene **Marine Invertebrates department**, where cabinets of corals, shells and sea fans are enhanced by the sound of waves breaking on a shore.

Earth Galleries

Head through Waterhouse Way towards the museum's other main section: the Earth Galleries. This section is brought to life by exciting special effects and atmospheric sound and lighting. A central escalator transports visitors into a gigantic rotating globe. At the top, the **Restless Surface** section looks at earthquakes and volcanoes. The tremors of an earthquake are simulated in a mock-up of a Japanese mini-market; and a bank of television sets next to a car covered in volcanic ash replays news reports of the 1991 eruption of Mt Pinatubo in the Philippines.

In **From the Beginning**, the story of the universe is told, from the time of the Big Bang 15,000 million years ago to the end of the solar system, which is pencilled in for 5,000 million years from now. Finally, demonstrating the sheer beauty our planet has to offer, is the **Earth's Treasury** gallery, which displays rocks, gems and minerals glittering in semi-darkness.

SCIENCE MUSEUM

Just around the corner on Exhibition Road is the third museum developed after the success of the 1851 Great Exhibition, the **Science Museum ❸** (tel: 0870-870 4771; www.science museum.org.uk; daily 10am–6pm;

free). This museum traces the history of inventions from the first steam train to the space rocket and has more than 10,000 exhibits, plus additional attractions such as an Imax cinema.

Ground Floor

The museum's ground floor is home to **Exploring Space** and **Making the Modern World**. The former's highlight is a replica of the *Apollo 11* lunar excursion module, but look out also for the videos of early rocket experiments in the 1920s.

Making the Modern World (with 'modern' defined as post-1750) brings together many of the museum's prize exhibits. Here you can find the world's oldest surviving steam locomotive, *Puffing Billy* (*c.*1815), Stephenson's pioneering *Rocket* passenger locomotive (1829) and the battered *Apollo 10* command module (1969).

Third Floor

Head up to the third floor for the magnificent **Flight Gallery**, with exhibits ranging from a seaplane to a Spitfire to hot-air balloons. Here too is the 1919 Vickers Vimy, in which Alcock & Brown made the first non-

Above: attractions at the Science Museum include: the Energy Hall, dominated by a 1903 mill engine; the Making of the Modern World, with a Lockheed Electra airliner hanging in silvery splendour from the ceiling; and the Exploring Space gallery, with a huge Spacelab 2 x-ray telescope – as used on the Space Shuttle.

Harrods' Motto

The store boasts that it can find any item you want and send it anywhere in the world, with the motto 'Everything for Everyone Everywhere'. Under this remarkable policy, Noël Coward was bought an alligator for Christmas, former US president Ronald Reagan was given a baby elephant, and highly unusual items, such as your very own wax model by Madame Tussauds, can be made a reality (albeit with the rather hefty price tag of around £250,000).

stop transatlantic flight, and a Messerschmitt rocket-propelled fighter, as well as the first British jet aircraft, the Gloster Whittle E28/39. Visitors can peer into the cockpit of a Douglas DC3 and participate in interactive exhibits illustrating the principles of flight. A flight simulator offers a rodeo-style ride (charge).

Past and Future

Now go back downstairs to the basement. As well as a child-oriented area, it houses the **Secret Life of the Home**, a collection of domestic appliances and gadgets that provoke nostalgia in adults and disbelief in children. A range of models charts the development of the electric toaster since 1923. Other everyday items include a 1925 Sol hairdryer and a 1945 Goblin Teasmade.

Other exhibits geared more towards adults include **Energy: Fuelling the Future**, **Health Matters**, **Glimpses of Medical History** and **Psychology: Mind Your Head**, while the games of **In Future** raise intriguing questions for everyone. Meanwhile, through manipulation of air and motion, the **SimEx Simulator** (charge) creates the sensory effect of, among other things, a dinosaur breathing down your neck.

KNIGHTSBRIDGE

End the route by walking east along Cromwell Road, which then turns into the Brompton Road. Note, on your left, **Brompton Oratory** ❹ (Thurloe Place; tel: 020-7808 0900; www.brompton oratory.com; daily 6.30am–8pm; free), a flamboyant Italian Baroque church designed by 29-year-old architect Herbert Gribble. Opposite is a good option for French cuisine, **Racine**, see ⑪③.

Department Stores

Now head up Brompton Road towards Knightsbridge station. At Nos 87–135, is the famous department store, **Harrods** ❺ (tel: 020-7730 1234; Mon–Sat 10am–8pm, Sun noon–6pm). East End grocer Henry Charles Harrod opened a store here in 1849, in anticipation of trade sparked by the Great Exhibition. The Harrod family sold the company in 1889, but the store still flourished. Construction of the current building, by C.W. Stephens, architect of Claridge's hotel, started in 1901. The Fayed brothers bought the store in 1983, and sold it to the Qatari royal family in 2010.

Highlights include the magnificent Art Nouveau food hall, a good place to buy provisions for a picnic in nearby Hyde Park *(see p.72)*, just north of Knightsbridge. Alternatively, if you want to carry on shopping, continue east on Knightsbridge to the up-market **Harvey Nichols** ❻ department store, or walk south down Sloane Street, which is lined with designer names and leads to the King's Road and Chelsea *(see opposite)*.

Food and Drink 🍴

③ RACINE

239 Brompton Road; tel: 020-7584 4477; www.racine-restaurant.com; daily L and D; £££

Behind the smart glass exterior classic French fare is cooked with panache. The three-course set menu, available till 7.30pm, offers very good value for this part of town.

CHELSEA

A summer afternoon in Chelsea might include a visit to London's oldest garden or the home of a famous writer, followed by a walk along the Thames or one of the capital's most famous shopping streets.

Riverside Chelsea was little more than a fishing village until around the 15th century, when it became fashionable with aristocrats who built smart country houses along the King's Road, which was then the private royal route linking Westminster with the palace of Hampton Court to the west.

In the 19th and 20th centuries the area drew artists enticed by the riverside setting and quality of the light. The 1960s marked the peak of its fame, but in the 1980s the area still had some edge, reflected by the opening of Vivienne Westwood and Malcolm McLaren's cult shop, Sex, at 430 King's Road.

Although Westwood's shop, renamed World's End (the name of the part of Chelsea west of the kink in the King's Road) is still there, the area is now far from cutting-edge; instead, it is one of the smartest, and most expensive, parts of London, and the domain of the well-heeled 'Sloane Ranger' *(see right)*.

SLOANE SQUARE

Start by the tube, on the eastern side of **Sloane Square ❶**, laid out in the late 18th century and named after Sir Hans Sloane, a wealthy physician and collector who purchased the manor of Chelsea in 1712. To your right is the **Royal Court Theatre** (tel: 020-7565

DISTANCE 3¾ miles (6km)
TIME Half to a full day
START/END Sloane Square
POINTS TO NOTE
This walk is best done on a summer's afternoon, when Chelsea Physic Garden and Carlyle's House are open. Note, also, that Saturdays are very busy on the King's Road.

5000; www.royalcourttheatre.com), dating from 1870. This is where John Osborne's mould-breaking *Look Back in Anger* was first staged in 1956, and it still has a reputation for staging high-quality new material. The café here, see ⓣ① *(p.82)*, is also very good.

Above from far left:
Harrods food hall;
Chelsea Pensioners.

Sloane Ranger
Commonly used since the 1960s, this term for the stereotypical preppie young Chelsea inhabitant became official in 1982, when society magazine *Harpers & Queen* published *The Official Sloane Ranger Handbook*.

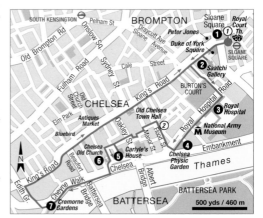

The Chelsea Flower Show

One of the largest of its kind in the world, the Chelsea Flower Show is a great social event, held in the gardens of the Royal Hospital in May each year. First held in 1862, the Royal Horticultural Society show includes numerous exhibition gardens

Peacock Ban

When the Pre-Raphaelite artist Dante Gabriel Rossetti and poet Swinburne lived at 16 Cheyne Walk, they kept peacocks in their garden. The birds so disturbed their neighbours that every lease on the row now prohibits tenants from keeping them.

Walk along the south side of the square now, and note to your right the reputable department store, **Peter Jones** (part of the John Lewis chain). Its architects have managed the transition from square to street in a sensuous curve.

DUKE OF YORK SQUARE

Continue west on the King's Road. On your left is Duke of York Square, a pedestrian enclave of up-market homeware and fashion units, cafés and, in winter, an ice rink. Partridges the grocers organises a regular Saturday food market outside their shop, with lots of enticing things to eat. Behind is the Duke of York's Headquarters, formerly a military campus, but now the home of the **Saatchi Gallery ❷** (tel: 020-7823 2363 ; www.saatchi-gallery.co.uk; daily 10am–6pm; free), showcasing contemporary art collected by former advertising mogul Charles Saatchi. He

was an early purchaser of work by YBAs (Young British Artists) such as Damien Hirst and Tracey Emin.

ROYAL HOSPITAL

Back on the King's Road, you must resist the temptation to shop in its many fashion and shoe stores and take the next left, Cheltenham Terrace. At the end, continue on to Franklin's Row, which joins Royal Hospital Road.

In front of you is the **Royal Hospital Chelsea ❸** (tel: 020-7881 5200; www.chelsea-pensioners.org.uk; Mon–Fri 10am–noon and 2–4pm; free), a grand building inspired by the Hôtel des Invalides in Paris and built by Christopher Wren in 1692. This is home to approximately 400 Chelsea Pensioners, retired war veterans who are identifiable by their red uniform coats. Next to the hospital is the **National Army Museum** (tel: 020-7881 2455; www.nam.ac.uk; daily 10am–5.30pm; free).

CHELSEA PHYSIC GARDEN

Continue west along Royal Hospital Road until you reach No. 66 and the **Chelsea Physic Garden ❹** (tel: 020-7352 5646; www.chelseaphysicgarden.co.uk; Apr–Oct Tue–Fri noon–5pm, Sun noon–6pm; charge); the entrance is on the left, on Swan Walk. Founded by the Society of Apothecaries in 1676, it is second only to the one in Oxford as the oldest botanic garden in the country. It has thousands of rare and unusual plants, and themed trails for children and adults.

Food and Drink 🍴

① ROYAL COURT

Royal Court Theatre; tel: 020-7565 5058; www.royalcourt theatre.com; Mon–Sat L and D; ££
The Royal Court's roomy ambient vaulted café is tucked away in what was the 19th-century theatre 'pit'. Slouch on the sofas with a drink, graze on tapas (some straight from Borough Market) or try the generous main dishes (served until 8pm). There's a limited wine selection, but try a glass of the well-priced Prosecco.

② COOPERS ARMS

87 Flood Street; tel: 020-7376 3120; www.coopersarms.co.uk; daily L and D; ££
This upper-crust London pub serves hearty portions of British classics, such as steak-and-kidney pie and bangers and mash, to a genteel Chelsea crowd.

CARLYLE'S HOUSE

At the end of Royal Hospital Road you come to Flood Street, where Margaret and Denis Thatcher once lived at No. 19. Head to the right for the excellent **Coopers Arms**, see ⑪②. From the pub, go west through the area's network of pretty streets – along Alpha Place, over Chelsea Manor Street on to Oakley Gardens, then west on Phene Street and Upper Cheyne Row – to Cheyne Row itself.

Here, at No. 24, time seems to stand still in **Carlyle's House ⑤** (tel: 020-7352 7087; www.nationaltrust.org.uk; Mar–Oct Wed–Sun 11am–5pm; charge). The Scottish historian Thomas Carlyle brought his wife Jane to live in this elegant Queen Anne house in 1834.

Their home was turned into a museum in 1896 and remains a time capsule of Victorian life, with papered-over panelling and books, furniture and pictures just as the Carlyles left them. What the 'Sage of Chelsea' did not find here was peace and quiet. His soundproofed attic study, built on the roof, failed to keep out the noise of cocks crowing, street musicians, and horses' hooves.

CHEYNE WALK

At the north end of Cheyne Row turn left into Upper Cheyne Row and Lawrence Street, home of the Chelsea porcelain works from 1745–84. Dr Johnson fancied his hand at the wheel, but his pots never survived the firing. Continue on to Cheyne Walk, one of London's most exclusive streets. Past residents include George Eliot, J.M.W. Turner, Dante Gabriel Rossetti *(see margin)* and, more recently, Mick Jagger.

Here, you will be confronted by a lumpen, gilded statue of Sir Thomas More, another famous resident. Henry VIII's chancellor went to the Tower, and was beheaded in 1535, having prepared his resting place in **Chelsea Old Church ⑥**. The building was nearly destroyed by a landmine in 1941 but was reassembled from the shattered fragments. Look out for the two carved capitals by Holbein.

Cremorne Gardens

The riverside walk here is attractive, with the sun on the water and houseboats moored by Battersea Bridge, but the road turns away from the river at **Cremorne Gardens ⑦**. In Victorian times, party-goers used to dance the night away beneath the coloured lanterns.

BACK TO SLOANE SQUARE

Edith Grove on the right will take you back to the King's Road. A brisk 25-minute walk past its shops (excluding stops) will take you to Sloane Square; alternatively, catch bus Nos 11 or 22 heading east. As you make your way back, look out, on your left, for Terence Conran's renovated Bluebird Garage, at No. 350 and, on the right, halfway along the King's Road, the Old Chelsea Town Hall, a popular spot for celebrity marriages. Flanking the town hall are two antiques markets.

Above from far left: 'Cardinal Vaughan' peony, Chelsea Flower Show; smart houses near Cheyne Walk; wedding car outside Chelsea Town Hall; toiletries at Jo Malone, King's Road.

Above: gourmet quiches at the Duke of York Square market; bedding and velvet slippers at the Designers Guild on the King's Road.

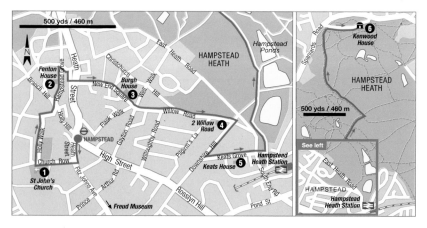

HAMPSTEAD

Full of pretty houses on leafy groves and set against the backdrop of its glorious heath, Hampstead seems the quintessence of an English village. In reality, it is not so much rural idyll as exclusive suburb, a haven in a hectic city.

Freud Museum
Walk south on Heath Street and Fitzjohn's Avenue, turn right at Nutley Terrace and left on to Maresfield Gardens for Sigmund Freud's house (tel: 020-7435 2002; www.freud.org.uk; Wed–Sun noon–5pm; charge). All is just as the psycho-analyst left it, including his couch.

DISTANCE 2¾ miles (4.5km)
TIME Half a day
START/END Hampstead tube
POINTS TO NOTE

It is best to walk this route between Wednesday and Sunday, when all the museums are open. Note that Kenwood House is about 15–20 minutes' walk from Hampstead tube.

Until not so long ago, Hampstead was the home of artists, writers and anyone with a liberal disposition. At the last count, the suburb had more than 90 blue plaques commemorating such famous residents as John Constable, George Orwell, Florence Nightingale and Sigmund Freud. Now, you only need to

have deep pockets to live here: its pretty alleys, leafy streets and heath make this villagey suburb a desirable address.

From **Hampstead tube station**, take Heath Street south (past **The Horseshoe**, see ①①) and turn right at Church Row, a street of Georgian houses. Follow the sign to John Constable's grave in the bosky graveyard of **St John's Church ①**, halfway down.

FENTON HOUSE

Head north up Holly Walk, past the one-time home of Scottish writer Robert Louis Stevenson, and turn left to Hampstead Grove. On your left is **Fenton House ②** (Windmill Hill; tel: 020-7435 3471; www.nationaltrust.org.uk; Mar–Oct Wed–Sun 11am–5pm;

charge), a grand William-and-Mary mansion built for a merchant. Behind gilded gates, the walled garden, with apple orchard and rose beds, has hardly changed for 300 years. Inside are fine paintings, furniture, porcelain and a collection of harpsichords. In spring, concerts recreate 18th-century parties.

BURGH HOUSE

Back on Hampstead Grove, turn right and descend the steps to Heath Street, then cross over to New End. At the far end of the street is New End Square and **Burgh House** ❸ (tel: 020-7431 0144; www.burghhouse.org.uk; Wed–Fri and Sun noon–5pm; free). Built in 1704, it contains the local history museum, with a display on painter John Constable and maps showing the location of 166 homes of celebrated residents.

Almost opposite the museum is the turning for Flask Walk, a pleasant detour taking you past boutiques and galleries to **The Flask**, see ⑪②.

WILLOW ROAD AND KEATS HOUSE

Returning to New End, continue on to Willow Road. At the far end, overlooking the heath, is the Modernist **2 Willow Road** ❹ (tel: 020-7435 6166; www.nationaltrust.org.uk; Mar–Oct Wed–Sun 11am–5pm; charge), designed by Hungarian-born architect Ernö Goldfinger for himself. Inside is his art collection, with works by Henry Moore, Bridget Riley, Max Ernst and Marcel Duchamp.

Next, turn right on Downshire Hill, then left on to Keats Grove to **Keats House** ❺ (tel: 020-7435 2062; www.keatshouse.cityoflondon.gov.uk; May–Oct Tue–Sun 1–5pm, Nov–Mar Fri–Sun only; charge), the Regency villa where the poet lodged before departing for Rome, where he died a year later, in 1821, aged 25. Under a plum tree in the garden he penned one of his best-loved poems, *Ode to a Nightingale*. Inside are his keepsakes of Fanny Brawne, the neighbour with whom he fell in love.

HAMPSTEAD HEATH

At the end of Keats Grove, turn left on to South End Road and take one of the paths on the right on to the heath. Bear north up the hill to **Kenwood House** ❻ (tel: 020-8348 1286; www.english-heritage.org.uk; daily 11.30am–4pm; free). This mansion was bequeathed to the nation by brewing magnate, Edward Guinness, and houses his art collection, with works by Rembrandt, Vermeer, Reynolds and Turner. It also contains some of Robert Adam's finest interiors. Outside again, stroll across the heath to return to Hampstead tube station.

Food and Drink

① THE HORSESHOE
28 Heath Street; tel: 020-7431 7206; daily L and D; ££–£££
Good real ales (it has its own microbrewery) and classic British food: lamb and beef dishes, then trifle or fruit crumble and custard.

② THE FLASK
14 Flask Walk; tel: 020-7435 4580; Mon–Sat L and D, Sun L; ££
Typical Victorian pub: comfortable and with two bars at the front separated by a fine 1880s glazed partition. Classic pub food.

NOTTING HILL

Notting Hill's appeal derives from its fusion of cultures and lifestyles – Rasta meets pasta, bourgeois splendour combines with bohemian chic. The best time to come is on a Saturday when Portobello Road market is in full swing.

What's in a Name?
Before *c*.1850, Portobello Road was a country lane snaking through hay fields and orchards. Its name derives from that of a nearby pig farm, which in turn was named after an English victory over Spain at Puerto Bello in the Gulf of Mexico in 1739.

DISTANCE 2 miles (3km)
TIME Half a day
START Notting Hill Gate tube
END Westbourne Park tube
POINTS TO NOTE

The Saturday market on Portobello Road gets extremely crowded by mid-morning, so arrive very early to snap up the bargains. There are also some stalls on Fridays and Sundays. If, on reaching Westway flyover, you want to escape the throng, Ladbroke Grove tube station is off to the left.

Notting Hill became fashionable in the 1990s, when monied people from the worlds of fashion and media moved in, attracted by the lingering street cred of the mix of ethnic cultures and shabby chic look. The neighbourhood is now extremely expensive and largely the province of investment bankers.

Go back in time, however, and it is a very different story. In the 1800s, when the area's grand crescents sat next to noxious slums, it was, according to Dickens, 'a plague spot scarcely equalled for its insalubrity by any other in London'. As recently as the 1950s, the district was very poor. Large numbers of Afro-Caribbean immigrants settled in overcrowded lodging houses, and the area saw race riots in 1958.

Now different cultures rub along more happily, though the local population has become largely white middle class, and the famous Notting Hill Carnival has grown from modest beginnings in the 1960s to become the world's second largest, after the one in Rio.

PORTOBELLO ROAD

Leaving **Notting Hil Gate tube station**, turn right (north) off Notting Hill Gate on to Pembridge Road. Walk past the retro shops and turn left into Por-

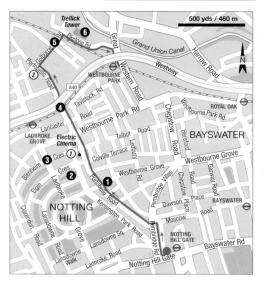

tobello Road. The top part of the road is largely residential, with pretty terraces painted different colours. Look for the blue plaque at No. 22, where the writer George Orwell used to live.

Street Market
Further down, beyond the turning for **Westbourne Grove ❶**, you enter the thick of the market for antiques and collectables. Dozens of stalls are hidden away in arcades such as the Admiral Vernon, on your left. Many are open only on Saturdays, when the streets are thronged with vendors hawking toast racks and teddy bears, plant pots and Ming vases. Bargaining is expected.

At the **Elgin Crescent ❷** turning, the theme changes to food, with traditional green grocery sitting side by side with organic olive bread. Behind stalls of pak choi and ciabatta, on your left at No. 191, is the **Electric Cinema** (tel: 020-7908 9696; www.the-electric.co.uk), which screens current films in a vintage setting, with leather armchairs, foot rests and wine coolers.

Further up, turn left down **Blenheim Crescent ❸** for **Books for Cooks** (tel: 020-7221 1992; www.booksforcooks.com: Tue–Sat 10am–6pm) at No. 4, a delightful little shop that is, of course, devoted to cookery books, but also offers cookery workshops and has a small café where you can sample the results.

Beyond the Westway
Back on Portobello Road, walk under the concrete **Westway flyover ❹**, where the market becomes a showcase for boho fashion. Boutiques in Portobello Green Arcade sell pink heart-shaped sunglasses and fake fur gilets, while stalls outside sell vintage clothes, old LPs and retro design.

Towards Golborne Road
Continuing to the end of Portobello Road, look out on your left for the **Galicia**, see ⑪①, a good place for lunch or tapas. This will bring you to the junction with **Golborne Road ❺**, where you should turn right. Here, Moroccan shops sell slippers and spices, and the Portuguese community queues for coffee, cakes and custard tarts at the **Lisboa** ⑪② at No. 57, and *bacalao* (dried salt cod) at the deli opposite. At the end of the road looms **Trellick Tower ❻**, designed by Ernö Goldfinger, after whom James Bond's old adversary was named. Turn right on Elkstone Road for the tube station.

Food and Drink 🍴
① THE GALICIA
323 Portobello Road; tel: 020-8969 3539; daily L and D; ££
Chaotic tapas bar and restaurant serving the local Spanish community. Tasty, unpretentious, authentic dishes, such as good rich stews, and some very tempting puddings.

② LISBOA PÂTISSERIE
57 Golborne Road, W10; tel: 020-8968 5242; daily 8am–7.30pm; £
If you fancy a snack, or a sugar rush, stop for a coffee and a pastry, or an authentic *pastel de nata* (a delicious custard tart) in the tiled interior of this popular and always bustling little Portuguese café.

Above from far left: houses on Portobello Road; antiques shop on Portobello Road; Notting Hill Carnival.

Carnival
On the August bank holiday each year, the streets of Notting Hill are packed with around a million people celebrating the massive three-day Caribbean festival. The first carnival, a small affair, was held in St Pancras Town Hall in 1959 to unite communities after race riots; it moved to Notting Hill in 1965. The main carnival days are the Sunday and Monday, but if you visit on Saturday night you can hear the steel bands practise.

Below: Notting Hill and Portobello Road are popular among the fashion crowd.

THE EAST END

Where once were slums, race riots and Jack the Ripper are now art galleries, trendy bars and urban cool, while in Canary Wharf, once the docks of Britain's imperial trade, is the power-architecture of investment banks.

Women's Library

Turn right as you leave Aldgate East Tube for the turning for Old Castle Street and the Women's Library (tel: 020-7320 2222; Tue–Fri 9.30am–5pm, Sat 10am–4pm; free). Converted from a Victorian bathhouse, it documents the history of women's rights, suffrage and sexuality.

DISTANCE 2½ miles (4km)

TIME A full day

START Whitechapel Art Gallery

END Geffrye Museum

POINTS TO NOTE

To attend the markets in full swing at Petticoat Lane, Spitalfields or Columbia Road, walk this route on a Sunday. Note also the very limited opening times of Dennis Severs' House *(see opposite).*

Long associated with poverty, overcrowding and inner-city grime, the increasingly gentrified East End is now under the spotlight as the location of the 2012 Olympic Games, held in Stratford. As well as being home to its indigenous cockneys, the area has historically also been the first stopping-point for immigrants in London and hosts a wide range of ethnicities. Its cultural mix, edgy atmosphere and once-cheap accommodation have also made it popular with artists in the last few decades. Meanwhile, over in the Docklands, it is the investment bankers who have moved in, housed in skyscrapers and posh riverside apartments on the former docks, once so vital to Britain's imperial trade.

WHITECHAPEL

From Aldgate East tube station, follow the signs to the exit next to the **Whitechapel Art Gallery ❶** (tel: 020-7522 7888; www.whitechapel.org; Tue–Sun 11am–6pm, Thur until 9pm; free). The gallery was founded in 1897 by a vicar and his wife, who aimed to combat spiritual and economic poverty in the East End, and the building was designed by the Arts and Crafts architect Charles Harrison Townsend. Today, it mounts high-quality exhibitions of

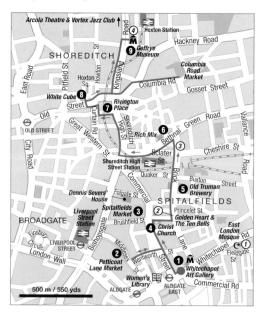

contemporary art. There is also an excellent café on the mezzanine level.

Leaving the gallery, turn right along Whitechapel Road to continue the route, or, if ready for lunch, turn left towards the **East London Mosque**, where Fieldgate Street, on your right, has some of London's best Pakistani restaurants, including **Tayyabs** ①①.

SPITALFIELDS

London's Old Markets

Just west of the Whitechapel Gallery, turn into Commercial Street on your right. Heading north, off to your left down Wentworth Street is **Petticoat Lane Market** ❷ (Mon–Fri and greatly expanded on Sun until 2pm), a centre of the rag trade for 400 years.

Further up Commercial Street, on your left, is **Spitalfields Market** ❸, formerly London's wholesale fruit and vegetable market (since 1682), and now hosting stalls selling fashions, jewellery, homewares, second-hand books and with organic food stalls on Sundays.

Eating and Drinking

On the other side of the road is **The Golden Heart** pub, renowned for its popularity among the BritArt crowd; the indulgent and eccentric landlady, Sandra Esquilant, was once voted the 80th most important person in the contemporary art world. The ghost of the Quaker prison reformer Elizabeth Fry is supposed to turn off beer taps in the cellar from time to time. A few doors along is **St John**, see ①②, and a little further still, on the corner of

Fournier Street, is **The Ten Bells** pub, where Jack the Ripper eyed up his victims before murdering them.

Christ Church Spitalfields

On the other corner of Fournier Street is **Christ Church** ❹ (tel: 020-7247 7202; www.christchurchspitalfields.org; Sun–Fri 11am–4pm; free), one of Nicholas Hawksmoor's finest works. It was built from 1714–29 to underline the power of the Church of England to the dissenting Huguenots who had settled in the area after fleeing Catholic France. Walking down Fournier Street you pass the fine houses the Huguenots built once they had grown wealthy from silk weaving and silver smithing.

Brick Lane – 'The Curry Mile'

At the end of the street, turn left on to Brick Lane, famous for its cheap curry

---

Food and Drink ①

① TAYYABS

83 Fieldgate Street; tel: 020-7247 9543; www.tayyabs.co.uk; daily L and D; £

Chaotic, often long queues, but good food (and prices). Delicious Seekh kebabs – succulent and tasty. Bring your own alcohol (no corkage).

② ST JOHN BREAD AND WINE

94–6 Commercial Street; tel: 020-7251 0848; www.stjohnbreadand wine.com; B, L and D daily; £££

Offshoot of the St John restaurant in Smithfields, similar but slightly cheaper. Fresh British produce using chef Fergus Henderson's concept of nose-to-tail eating. Oysters, pig's head and radishes, smoked eel and pickled prunes, fennel and Berkswell cheese.

Above from far left: Lamb Street at Spitalfields Market; find traditional British produce at A. Gold on Brushfield Street; Dennis Severs' house; hearty Old Spot chop at St John Bread and Wine.

18 Folgate Street

Two streets beyond Spitalfields Market is the 18th-century time warp of Dennis Severs' House (tel: 020-7247 4013; www.dennissevers house.co.uk; Sun noon–4pm, Mon following first and third Sun of month noon–2pm; Mon nights by candlelight; booking required; charge). In 1967, Severs moved from his native California and bought this silk weaver's house. Living with no electricity or modern appliances, he recreated its 18th-century state. It is now as if the original family have just left the room, leaving a half-eaten scone and a smouldering fire.

Above from left: hanging out on Brick Lane; Columbia Road flower market; White Cube art gallery; seamstress on Brick Lane, reflecting the increasingly creative slant of the area and its connections with the rag trade.

Flower Market On Sundays between 8am and 2pm, Columbia Road is taken over by a flower market. Have a mooch, bide your time in a café, and at the end of the session the remaining plants and flowers are sold off cheaply. Street music provided by busking bands.

houses, thanks to another immigrant community, this time the Bangladeshis.

Crossing Brick Lane is Princelet Street, with some fine early 18th-century houses intact *(see margin, right)*. Further up is the **Old Truman Brewery 5**, which houses shops, studios, bars, restaurants, nightclubs and, on Sundays, a craft market. Towards the end of the street, among the boutiques and cafés of this now-fashionable area, is a much-loved relic of its once sizeable Jewish community – **Beigel Bake**, see ⑪③, on your left.

HOXTON AND SHOREDITCH

At the top of Brick Lane, turn left on to Bethnal Green Road. On your right is **Rich Mix 6** (tel: 020-7613 7490; www.richmix.org.uk; daily 9am–11pm), a former garment factory, which now houses a cinema, art galleries and

recording studios. Just beyond is the crossroads with Shoreditch High Street, where you turn right.

This area was very heavily bombed during World War II, and suffered severe depopulation thereafter – by 1960, St Leonard's Church on the High Street had no parishoners left. Regeneration only took root in the 1990s, when artists moved in, attracted by the cheap studio space. With their success, galleries, bars and nightclubs followed – and higher prices.

Rivington Place

Located on your left, just off the High Street, is Rivington Street. On the right is London's newest public gallery, **Rivington Place 7** (tel: 020-7749 1240; www.rivingtonplace.org; Tue–Sat 11am–6pm, Thur until 9pm; charge). Devoted to cultural diversity, the building hosts art exhibitions and

Food and Drink 🍴

③ BEIGEL BAKE
159 Brick Lane; tel: 020-7729 0616; 24 hours daily; £
Perfect plump, soft beigels. Fillings of smoked salmon, cream cheese, herring, or, best of all, salt beef carved off the joint in front of you. Good with mustard and gherkins. Also onion platzels, chollah bread, and stupendous cakes. All very cheap. Cheerful staff.

④ SÔNG QUÊ
134 Kingsland Road; tel: 020-7613 3222; www.songque.co.uk; L and D daily; £
Vietnamese restaurant with a huge menu (28 types of noodle soup). Fresh, aromatic food. Friendly service.

Right: period room in the Geffrye Museum.

film screenings. Its latticed facade was inspired by a Sowei tribal mask.

Hoxton Square

At the end of Rivington Street, turn right on to Curtain Road and left on to Old Street. The first turning on your right is for Hoxton Square. It was here that playwright Ben Jonson killed Gabriel Spencer in a duel in 1598. Today it is a focus of the contemporary art scene in the East End and a fashionable nightlife spot. Immediately on your left is **White Cube** ❽ (tel: 020-7930 5373; www.whitecube.com; Tue–Sat 10am–6pm; free), the art gallery that sells the work of Damien Hirst, Tracey Emin and the Chapman brothers.

A detour off the square to the left, past **Sh!**, a boudoir-style women-only sex shop, brings you to Pitfield Street. At No. 17 is **Bookartbookshop**, selling limited-edition artists' books, while at No. 45 is a relic of tatty old Hoxton: **Charlie Wright's International Bar** (tel: 020-7490 8345; daily until the small hours), where the eponymous former weight-lifter presides over his dive of a bar, where you can listen to jazz or dance to 1980s tracks.

Geffrye Museum

Returning to Old Street, head east, and at the crossroads turn left on to Kingsland Road. (On Sundays go straight on for the Flower Market on **Columbia Road**, the first right off Hackney Road – *see margin, left*.) Further up Kingsland Road, on your right is the **Geffrye Museum** ❾ (tel: 020-7739 9893; www.geffrye-museum.org.uk; Tue–Sat

10am–5pm, Sun noon–5pm; free). Housed in former almshouses, built in 1714, this interior-decoration museum first opened in 1914 as a resource and inspiration for workers in the East End furniture trade. It is set up as a series of period rooms taking you from 1600 to the present day. There is also a series of 'period gardens' outside.

Almost next door is the best of the area's many Vietnamese restaurants, see ⑪④. For evening entertainment, take a bus further up Kingsland Road for, on your left, the **Vortex Jazz Club** (tel: 020-7993 3643; www. vortexjazz.co.uk) and, tucked way on Ashwin Street off to the right, near Dalston Lane, the fringe-style **Arcola Theatre** (tel: 020-7503 1646; www.arcolatheatre.com).

19 Princelet Street

This unrestored 18th-century house was built by Huguenot master silk weavers. In the 19th century it was occupied by Polish Jews, who built a synagogue in the garden. Since the house is in a fragile state, it is only open occasionally. Call 020-7247 5352 for details, or check www.19princeletstreet .org.uk. When the building is stabilised, it is hoped that it will house a Museum of Immigration and Diversity.

The Docklands

From c.1700, London's docks grew as the hub of Britain's imperial trade, but in the 1960s their demise came quickly, as trade moved to the deep-water ports required for the new container shipping. By 1980, all London's docks were closed, leaving behind derelict land, unemployment and poverty. The 1990s brought regeneration, with the building of the capital's second major financial district, the Canary Wharf complex. Its main tower, at 800ft (244m), was Britain's tallest building until the Shard was built *(see p.60)*. Take a ride on the Docklands Light Railway (DLR) from Bank to Greenwich to get an idea of the mix of old and new, rich and poor, then visit the Museum in Docklands at West India Quay or Mudchute City Farm on Pier Street.

2012 OLYMPICS SITES

Britain is concentrating extraordinary efforts and money – over £9 billion – on the 2012 Olympics, and with immense public pressure for results, the investment looks set to achieve spectacular returns.

Floating Cinema

One of the quirkier side attractions of the 2012 Olympics is a narrowboat that has been cleverly adapted as a cinema by local architects. It will navigate the canals of the boroughs hosting the games and present on-board film screenings as well as larger open-air events on the canal banks. See www.floating cinema.info for further details.

START Olympic Park, Stratford
END Wembley Stadium
POINTS TO NOTE
While the London Underground is the easiest transport option, it may be the most crowded. Consider overground trains, buses and park-and-ride schemes. London will be very crowded, hotels heavily booked, and restaurants may be swamped. Book as far ahead as possible.

The 2012 Olympic Games (www. london2012.com) will take place from 27 July to 12 August, with the focus of attention on Olympic Park in Strat-ford, East London. There are also numerous other venues across the capital and across the country – from football at Old Trafford in Manchester to rowing at Eton Dorney. There is also the Paralympic Games from 29 August to 9 September. Thereafter, most of the venues will remain in use as part of the Olympics' legacy, and can still be visited, for sports activities or just to see the spectacular architecture and design.

THE OLYMPIC PARK

The **Olympic Park** ❶ itself is a vast site accommodating nine venues: the Olympic Stadium, Aquatics Centre, Water Polo Arena, Basketball Arena,

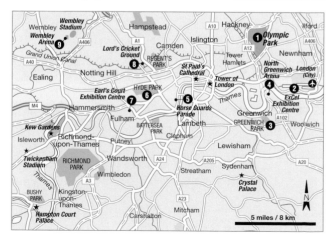

Handball Arena, Velodrome, BMX Track, Hockey Centre and Eton Manor (wheelchair tennis). Visitors can get there from central London by public transport; Stratford and Stratford International stations are on the east side of the park, and West Ham Station a short walk to the south. Overground trains run from London Liverpool Street, tube trains on the Jubilee and Central lines, and Docklands Light Railway (DLR) trains from Tower Gateway.

The centrepiece is the 80,000-capacity Olympic Stadium in the south of the Olympic Park, where the main track events will be staged. Sweeping away from the stadium are gardens that celebrate British horticulture with more than 250 species of plants. In the park's southeast corner is the Aquatics Centre, designed by Zaha Hadid, and already an iconic building. Another architectural feat is the Velodrome at the northern end of the site; this eco-friendly structure is clad in wood, and is 100 percent naturally ventilated.

DOCKLANDS AND GREENWICH

Elsewhere in London, the **ExCeL Exhibition Centre ❷** in Docklands (DLR to Custom House) will accommodate five arenas for a variety of sports, including boxing, fencing, judo, table tennis, weight-lifting and wrestling. Just across the river, the equestrian events benefit from the glorious setting of **Greenwich Park ❸**.

A little further to the east is the **North

Greenwich Arena ❹, formerly the Millennium Dome, which is hosting gymnastics (reached on the Jubilee line).

CENTRAL LONDON VENUES

In central London, there will be beach volleyball on **Horse Guards Parade ❺** in Westminster, and nearby, the marathons and cycling road races will start and finish on The Mall in front of Buckingham Palace. Fifteen minutes' walk north, in **Hyde Park ❻**, spectators can watch the triathlon – with a grandstand set up by the finishing area. A short underground ride west from Hyde Park Corner conveys volleyball fans to the **Earl's Court Exhibition Centre ❼** just outside tube station.

LORD'S AND WEMBLEY

In northwest London, the Jubilee line will ferry passengers to **Lord's Cricket Ground ❽** in St John's Wood, where the archery tournament is being staged. The same tube line (and the Metropolitan one) extends further north to **Wembley Arena ❾** for the badminton and rhythmic gymnastics events. Right next door, the 120,000-seat Wembley Stadium will stage the gold medal matches in the football competition.

Above from far left: artist's impression of how the Olympic Stadium will look; London 2012 medal design.

ArcelorMittal Orbit Anish Kapoor's sculptural tribute to the Olympics is 72ft (22m) higher than New York's Statue of Liberty, is made of over 1,400 tonnes of steel and has cost almost £20m. It is named after London's richest resident, Lakshmi Mittal, as it is sponsored by his steel company. Visitors will be able to ascend to the flying-saucer-style viewing platform and enjoy spectacular views over the Olympic Park and the city beyond.

Food and Drink

In addition to cafés and restaurants within the Olympic Park, the brand new Westfield Stratford City shopping centre next door has about 70 outlets, including branches of chains such as Jamie's Italian and Yo! Sushi, a gastropub called The Cow, and an offshoot of Balans bar and café (already a fixture in central London's Soho).

GREENWICH

Compared to central London, Greenwich has a stately but sedate feel. With buildings by Sir Christopher Wren and Inigo Jones, the royal park and a majestic river frontage, it evokes the full splendour of British maritime history.

St Alfege Church
This church was built by architect Nicholas Hawksmoor in 1714 on the site at which St Alfege, Archbishop of Canterbury, was killed by a raiding party of Danes in 1012. Inside are memorials to General Wolfe and composer Thomas Tallis.

DISTANCE 2 miles (3km)
TIME A full day
START *Cutty Sark*
END Greenwich Park
POINTS TO NOTE

To reach Greenwich, take a boat from Westminster or Tower of London pier (www.thamesriverservices.co.uk), or the Docklands Light Railway (DLR) to Cutty Sark station, or a mainline train from London Bridge.

Of the various ways to get to Greenwich, you could take a boat, just as Queen Elizabeth I used to do, in her state barge rowed from Whitehall to her palace here. The boat today drops you off by the *Cutty Sark* clipper, the starting point for this tour. The DLR also deposits you near the quayside. If you take the train, the *Cutty Sark* is five minutes' walk away – turn left on to Greenwich High Road and follow the road round as it veers left at St Alfege Church. The *Cutty Sark* soon comes into view, ahead to your right.

ALONG THE RIVER

The Cutty Sark

The **Cutty Sark** ❶ (tel: 020-8858 2698; www.cuttysark.org.uk) was a clipper that transported tea from China and, later, wool from Australia. Launched in Scotland in 1869, she was the last and fastest of these ships and finally retired in 1922. The ship's name comes from Robert Burns' poem, *Tam O'Shanter*, in which Tam meets a group of witches, all of whom are ugly, but for one, who is young and beautiful and wears only a 'cutty sark' – a short chemise or shirt; the ship's figurehead represents this witch. Unfortunately, while undergoing restoration in 2007, the ship was badly damaged by fire;

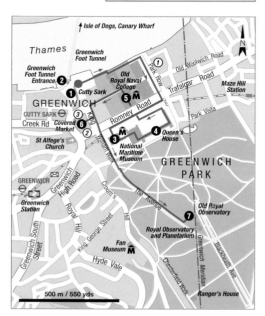

following a complete overhaul, it is due to reopen to the public in spring 2012.

Greenwich Foot Tunnel

Also on the river front is the round pavilion containing the entrance to the **Greenwich Foot Tunnel ❷** (daily dawn–dusk; free). The tunnel was completed in 1902 and allowed south London residents to walk to work at the docks on the Isle of Dogs on the north side of the river. Inside, a lift and a long spiral staircase take you down 50ft (15m) to the tunnel, lined with 200,000 glazed white tiles.

River Path

Now walk east along the river path past the two blocks of the **Royal Naval College**. The gap between them ensured that the Queen's House (to your right) had unobstructed views of the river. For similarly excellent views of the Thames, you could refuel at the **Trafalgar Tavern**, see ⑪①.

MARITIME MUSEUM

From Park Row, take a right turn at Romney Road and cross over to the **National Maritime Museum ❸** (tel: 020-8858 4422; www.nmm.ac.uk; daily 10am–5pm; free). The museum is formed from the Queen's House and two wings, joined by colonnades.

The public collection is housed in the larger west wing, with permanent displays on naval history, polar exploration, colonialism and oceanography. Highlights include the Royal Barge of 1732, decorated with lions, dragons and monsters; and the Nelson gallery (with the tunic he was wearing when fatally wounded at Trafalgar – you can even see the musket-ball hole). Short, free talks and tours are run throughout the day.

The west wing also now benefits from a large new extension, the Sammy Ofer Wing, which accommodates temporary exhibitions, a café, a rooftop restaurant and a shop.

Food and Drink ⑪
① TRAFALGAR TAVERN
6 Park Row; tel: 020-8858 2909; www.trafalgartavern.co.uk; daily L and D; ££
Historic pub built in 1837, where Victorian politicians including Gladstone and Disraeli used to celebrate the end of the parliamentary session with fish dinners. It was also popular with writers Thackeray, Wilkie Collins and Dickens, who set the wedding breakfast scene in *Our Mutual Friend* here. Bar food includes fried whitebait, cod and chips, and sausage and mash. The Collingwood Restaurant offers more formal meals.

Above from far left: the Royal Naval College; roof of the Covered Market.

Millennium Dome
Northeast of Greenwich is Britain's monument to the new millennium: a marquee-like structure in the shape of a convex watch face. From the outset the Dome was plagued by controversy, from its initial £750-million construction budget, numerous overspends and government bailouts, to its unclear function and meagre 25-year lifespan. It has since been renamed the O2 Arena and is now used as a venue for pop concerts.

Left: looking out of the chapel of the Old Royal Naval College.

Above from left:
Greenwich Park; Old
Royal Naval College
'Painted Hall' ceiling
and chapel ceiling;
Vanbrugh's house.

Fan Museum
At 12 Crooms Hill on
the western edge of
Greenwich Park is
the Fan Museum
(tel: 020-8305 1441;
www.fan-museum.org;
Tue–Sat 11am–5pm
Sun noon–5pm;
charge) containing
3,500 fans from
around the world,
dating from the 11th
century to the
present. Look for the
Fabergé *point de gaze*
lace fan surrounded
by rose diamonds. If
you can afford it, you
can commission your
own elaborate fan.

The Queen's House

Now walk along the colonnade to the **Queen's House ❹** (times as for the National Maritime Museum). Construction on this, England's first Palladian villa, began in 1616, to designs by Inigo Jones. Intended for James I's Queen Anne, it was only completed after her death, and was then given by Charles I to Henrietta Maria. She stayed here only briefly, as the Civil War broke out in 1642.

Today, the house is used to display the National Maritime Museum's art collection, with seascapes and portraits by, among others, Joshua Reynolds and Thomas Gainsborough. The real attraction, however, is the architecture, which is sublime and deceptively simple: the Tulip Stairs, for example, were the first centrally unsupported spiral stairs constructed in England.

Food and Drink 🍴

② BAR DU MUSÉE

17 Nelson Road; tel: 020-8858 4710; www.bardumusee.com; daily Br, L and D; £££
An atmospheric bar that was previously an antiques shop, and behind it a restaurant with a garden providing outside seating in summer. Bistro-style food. Service can be a little slow.

③ ADMIRAL HARDY

7 College Approach, Greenwich; tel: 020-8858 6452; www.admiralhardy. co.uk; daily L and D; ££
Comfortable pub built in 1830, and named after the admiral from whom Nelson received his dying kiss. Reasonable food, including roast beef and Yorkshire pudding on Sundays.

NAVAL COLLEGE

Now cross over the road again and enter the **Old Royal Naval College ❺** (tel: 020-8269 4747; daily grounds 8am–6pm, hall and chapel 10am–5pm; free) by the Romney Road Gate. Built on the site of the Tudor royal palace of Placentia (birthplace of Elizabeth I), the complex was founded in 1694 as a hospital for elderly and infirm seamen. Sir Christopher Wren was appointed architect, and laid out all the foundations early on, so that future architects would have to fulfil his master plan.

By the 19th century, British naval supremacy meant fewer casualties of war, and during the 1860s the hospital closed. In 1873 the Royal Naval College moved in; young officers were trained here until 1998, when the College passed to the Greenwich Foundation.

Today, only the 'Painted Hall' and the chapel are open to the public. The Painted Hall was originally intended as the dining room for the hospital. Unfortunately, Sir James Thornhill took so long to paint it (1707–26) and made it so elaborate (he was paid by the yard) that injured sailors never got to eat there, and it became a tourist attraction. In 1806, Admiral Lord Nelson's body lay in state here following his death at the Battle of Trafalgar; over three days, up to 30,000 people came to view the body.

The chapel, completed in 1789, is an unaltered example of the Greek-revival style of James 'Athenian' Stuart, with its classical columns and motifs. Worthy of contemplation inside is the altarpiece by

the American painter, Benjamin West; it depicts the story of St Paul's shipwreck on the island of Malta.

COVERED MARKET

Leave the Naval College grounds by the west side on to King William Walk and cross the road to the **Covered Market ❻** (www.greenwich-market. co.uk; Wed–Sun 10am–5.30pm). Here, you can browse the stalls selling food, jewellery, clothing, toiletries and gifts, as well as the shops alongside, or visit a pub or restaurant, see ⑪② and ⑪③.

GREENWICH PARK

From the Covered Market, return to King William Walk and head south, down the side of the Maritime Museum and through the gates into **Greenwich Park** (tel: 020-8858 2608; www.royalparks.org.uk; daily 6am–dusk; free).

Observatory and Planetarium
Follow the park's main road up the hill to the **Old Royal Observatory ❼** (tel: 020-8312 8565; www.nmm.ac.uk; daily 10am–5pm; free). Founded by Charles II in 1675 for the study of astronomy and the fixing of longitude, it was designed by Wren (an amateur astronomer) for Flamsteed, the Astronomer Royal, who lived and worked here until his death in 1719. Today, scientific instruments on display include sundials, atomic clocks, and Harrison's marine chronometers.

On the roof is a time ball, erected in 1833. At 12.55pm every day the ball rises up the pole, reaching the top at 12.58pm, and then dropping at exactly 1pm. The ball can be seen clearly from the river, and ships used to use it to check their time. In the courtyard below, brass strips set in the ground mark the **Greenwich Meridian**, the line dividing the eastern and western hemispheres.

Nearby is the South Building, housing the **Planetarium** (tel: 020-8312 8575; Mon–Fri 12.45–3.45pm, Sat–Sun and Aug daily 11am–1.30pm; shows every hour; charge).

After admiring the view, wander back to the town, though if you have children you may want to visit the boating pond and playground near the east wing of the Maritime Museum. Note, however, that during the 2012 Olympic Games, the park will host the equestrian events, and some of the usual facilities may be closed.

Vanbrugh's House
On the eastern edge of the park is a fortress-like folly, built in 1719 by Sir John Vanbrugh, the architect and dramatist, as his own residence while he was Surveyor to the Royal Naval Hospital. The castle is modelled on the French Bastille, where Vanbrugh was imprisoned as a British spy in 1690–2.

The Ranger's House

On the western edge of Greenwich Park, on Chesterfield Walk, is the Ranger's House (tel: 020-8853 0035; www.english-heritage. org.uk; Apr–Sept Sat–Wed 11.30am–4pm; charge). An elegant Georgian villa built in 1723, it became the official residence of the 'Ranger of Greenwich Park' after 1815, when the post was held by Princess Sophia Matilda, niece of George III. Today it houses the art collection of diamond magnate Sir Julius Wernher (1850–1912). Among the 700 items are early religious paintings, Dutch Old Masters, carved Gothic ivories, Renaissance bronzes and fine silver.

KEW

This southwest London suburb is synonymous with the 300-acre (120-hectare) royal botanic gardens, which contain, 30,000 types of plants, dozens of follies, glasshouses, lakes, ponds and even a Chinese pagoda. This route shows you some of its highlights and allows a leisurely ramble around the rest.

Steam Museum
Across the river from Kew Gardens is Kew Bridge Steam Museum (tel: 020-8568 4757; www.kbsm.org; Tue–Sun 11am–4pm; charge). Inside a Victorian waterworks are steam pumping engines, while outside is a narrow-gauge railway, which operates at weekends. To find the museum, follow Kew Road north, cross the bridge, turn left on to Kew Bridge Road and then right on to Green Dragon Lane.

DISTANCE 2 miles (3km)
TIME Half to a full day
START/END Kew Gardens tube
POINTS TO NOTE
The best way to get to Kew from central London is by tube: buy a ticket for zone 3 and take a westbound train on the Richmond branch of the District line. From the tube station, Kew Gardens are a few minutes' walk up Station Parade and then Lichfield Road. Alternatively, take an overland train from Waterloo to Kew Bridge.

Food and Drink 🍴

① THE ORANGERY
Kew Gardens; tel: 020-8332 5686; www.kew.org; daily B, L and AT, 10am until an hour before gardens close; ££
Never successful as a hothouse for oranges (the light levels are too low), this classical building by Sir William Chambers is a fine setting for a restaurant, offering salads, pasta, sandwiches and cakes.

② MA CUISINE
9 Station Approach; tel: 020-8332 1923; www.macuisinebistrot.co.uk; daily B, L and D; £££
The best-value restaurant in the area (especially the lunch time set menus) recreates the classic French bistro experience.

In the leafy suburb of Kew are the **Royal Botanic Gardens** (tel: 020-8332 5655; www.kew.org.uk; Apr–Oct Mon–Fri 9.30am–6pm, Sat–Sun until 7.30pm, Nov–Mar 9.30am–4.15pm; glasshouses and museums close half an hour earlier than gardens; charge, children free). Passing into royal hands in the 1720s, the gardens were created by Prince Frederick, son of George II, in 1731. His widow, Augusta, introduced the botanical element in 1759, and the grounds were subsequently landscaped by that most renowned of all gardeners, 'Capability' Brown. Kew became famous, though, when the botanist Sir Joseph Banks returned in 1771 from his global travels with Captain Cook, bringing back many strange and exotic plants, and cultivating them in the royal gardens here.

PALM HOUSE AND LAKE

Enter the gardens by the **Victoria Gate ❶**, then pick up a map and head north towards the **Palm House ❷**, which fronts on to a lake. Designed by Decimus Burton, the Palm House was completed in 1848 and was the first large-scale wrought-iron structure of its kind. Each of its iridescent panes of glass is hand-blown. Inside, climb

up the spiral stairs through the steamy tropical atmosphere to the galleries and inspect the canopy of banana trees, coconuts and pawpaws.

In the basement is the **Marine Display**, with tanks of corals, fish, algae and mangrove swamps. Just to the side of the Palm House is the **Waterlily House ❸**, encompassing a circular pond covered in giant Amazonian water lilies.

Outside, on the opposite side of the lake, another Decimus Burton creation, the **Plants and People Museum ❹**, illustrates mankind's dependence on plants, with exhibits displayed in the museum's fine original Victorian mahogany cabinets.

PRINCESS OF WALES CONSERVATORY

Continuing northeast beyond the lake, follow the signs for the **Princess of Wales Conservatory ❺**. This glass-house is divided into 10 microclimates, suitable for everything from cacti to carnivorous plants. It is particularly worth seeking out the *titan arum* − equally renowned for being the world's largest flower, for its foul smell (like rotting flesh) and for its rare flowerings.

KEW PALACE

Next, heading northwest, take some refreshment at the **Orangery**, see ⑪①, en route to **Kew Palace ❻** (Apr–Oct daily 10am–4.15pm; charge). Originally built for a Dutch merchant, Britain's smallest palace was leased to Queen Caroline in 1728 for 'the rent of £100 and a fat Doe'. George III later bought the palace and recuperated here during his first period of madness. The garden behind is laid out in 17th-century style with parterres of box and herbs, ornamented with statuary.

If your time is up, retrace your steps to the tube. Those looking for a restaurant before the journey back to central London, might consider **Ma Cuisine**, see ⑪②, just off Station Parade.

Hampton Court
In summer, you could visit Kew Gardens in the morning and Hampton Court in the afternoon. Boats leave Kew at 11.30am, 12.30pm and 1pm for Hampton Court and return at 4pm, 4.30pm and 5pm. For more information and to check times, tel: 020-7930 2062; www.wpsa.co.uk.

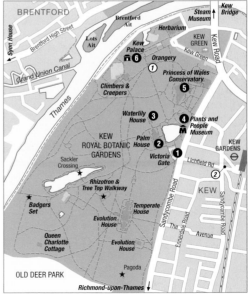

DIRECTORY

A user-friendly alphabetical listing of practical information, hand-picked hotels and restaurants, plus a taster of the city's nightlife, clearly organised by area, to suit all budgets and tastes.

A

AIRPORTS AND ARRIVAL

Airports

London has two major international airports: Heathrow, 15 miles (24km) to the west (mainly scheduled flights) and Gatwick, 25 miles (40km) to the south (scheduled and charter flights), plus three smaller airports, Stansted and Luton (north) and London City (east).

Heathrow: The fastest connection to central London is the Heathrow Express (tel: 0845-600 1515; www. heathrowexpress.com) to Paddington, every 15 minutes, 5am–11.30pm, taking 15 minutes. Paddington connects with several tube lines *(see map inside back cover)*. The fare is £16.50 single. A cheaper option is the 25-minute Heathrow Connect service, which stops at several stations; a single costs £8.50 (tel: 08457 484 950; www. heathrowconnect.com).

There is a direct tube route (www.tfl. gov.uk; £5 single) on the Piccadilly line, daily 5am (6am on Sun) until 11.40pm, 55 minutes to central London.

National Express (tel: 0871-781 8178, www.nationalexpress.com) runs coaches from Heathrow to Victoria; journey time 45–80 minutes, depending on traffic; single from £5.

Gatwick: The Gatwick Express (www.gatwickexpress.com) leaves Gatwick for Victoria every 15 minutes, 4.30am–12.30am. It takes 30 minutes and costs £18 one way. Also non-express services to Victoria, London Bridge and King's Cross. Singles from £12.50; 35–45 minutes.

Stansted: The Stansted Express rail link (www.stanstedexpress.com) goes to Liverpool Street every 15 minutes; journey time 45 minutes; a single costs £20.

London City: The DLR stop for London City is six minutes from Canning Town tube (Jubilee line); every 10 minutes from 5.30am–1.15am.

Luton: Luton Airport Parkway is linked by Thameslink services to King's Cross and Blackfriars, every 15 minutes, weekdays only; 40 minutes.

Arrival By Train

Eurostar services from Paris Gare du Nord take around 2¼ hours; from Brussels 2 hours, to London St Pancras. For UK bookings, tel: 0870-518 6186; www.eurostar.com.

Vehicles are carried by **Le Shuttle** (tel: 08705-353 535; www.eurotunnel.com) through the tunnel between Folkestone in Kent and Sangatte in France. Two–five departures each hour, and the trip takes 35 minutes. Bookings not essential, but advisable at peak times. Fares vary according to time of travel: late at night or early morning are usually cheaper. Taking a car (with any number of passengers) through the tunnel costs from about £44 single.

C

CHILDREN

Public Transport: Up to four children aged 11 or under can travel free on the

Airport Numbers
Heathrow:
tel: 0844-335 1801.
Gatwick:
tel: 0844-335 1802.
Stansted:
tel: 0844-335 1803.
London City:
tel: 020-7646 0088.
Luton:
tel: 01582-405 100

underground if accompanied by an adult. Eleven to 15-year-olds can get much reduced off-peak travel but need an Oyster photocard; buses are free for under 16s, but 11–15year-olds need an Oyster photocard, see www.tfl.gov.uk/tickets for details.

Supplies: Infant formula and nappies (diapers) can be found in chemists (pharmacies) and supermarkets. If you require over-the-counter medications such as Calpol (liquid paracetamol) late at night, Bliss Pharmacy (5 Marble Arch; tel: 020-7723 6116) is open daily until midnight.

CRIME

Hold on to purses, do not put wallets in back pockets, and do not place handbags on the ground in busy restaurants. Gangs of professional thieves target the tube. Use only licensed minicabs and black cabs.

In an emergency, dial 999 from any phone (free). Otherwise telephone the nearest police station, listed under 'Police' in the telephone directory.

CUSTOMS REGULATIONS

There are no official restrictions on the movement of goods within the European Union (EU), provided those goods were purchased within the EU. However, British Customs (www.hmrc.gov.uk) have set the following personal-use 'guide levels': 3,200 cigarettes or 400 cigarillos or 200 cigars or 3kg tobacco (200 cigarettes or 250g of smoking tobacco if coming from

eastern European countries); 10 litres spirits, 20 litres fortified wines, 90 litres wine, 110 litres beer.

Those entering from a non-EU state are subject to these limits: 200 cigarettes or 100 cigarillos or 50 cigars or 250g of tobacco; 2 litres still table wine plus 1 litre spirits (over 22 percent by volume) or 2 litres fortified or sparkling wine or other liqueurs; 60 ml of perfume plus 250 ml of toilet water; £145 worth of gifts, souvenirs or other goods.

There are no restrictions on the amount of currency you can bring in.

CYCLING

Route maps for cyclists are available from the London Cycling Campaign (www.lcc.org.uk) or London Cycle Network (www.londoncyclenetwork.org.uk). A bike lending scheme exists whereby you borrow a bike from one of dozens of docking stations all over central London, then leave it at any other docking station. No need to sign up first: just pay the access fee and usage charge at the docking station with a credit or debit card. See www.tfl.gov.uk for a map of locations.

D

DISABLED ACCESS

An excellent guidebook is *Access in London* by Gordon Couch, William Forrester and Justin Irwin (Quiller Press). The London Tourist Board also provides a free leaflet, *London For All*, available from Information Centres. For

Above from far left: children at the Natural History Museum; desirable London address.

Cycle Hire
Reputable bike-hire firms in London include: London Bicycle Tour Company (tel: 020-7928 6838; www.londonbicycle. com) and OY Bike (tel: 0845 226 5571; www.oybike.com).

details on public transport see www.dft.gov.uk/transportforyou/access/.

Artsline is a freephone information service for disabled people, covering the arts and entertainment (tel: 020-7388 2227; www.artsline.org.uk).

DRIVING

Unless you are planning on making several trips outside the capital, a car may be more of a hindrance than a help, and certainly a considerable expense, owing to the congestion charge *(see below)* and high parking costs.

If you do hire (or bring) a car, remember to drive on the left and observe speed limits (police detection cameras are common). It is strictly illegal to drink and drive, and penalties are severe. Drivers and passengers must wear seat belts. For further information consult the *Highway Code*.

Congestion Charge: In central London, drivers must pay a congestion charge. The boundaries of the congestion zone, which extends from Kensington in the west to the City in the east, are clearly indicated with signs and road markings. Cars entering this zone Mon–Fri 7am–6.30pm are filmed and drivers are fined if a payment of £8 has not been made by midnight the same day (or £10 the following day). You can pay at many newsagents and by phone or online (tel: 0845-900 1234; www.cclondon.com).

Fuel: Petrol (gasoline) is sold at filling stations and outside many supermarkets (priced in litres).

Parking: This is a big problem in central London. Meters are slightly less expensive than NCP (multistorey) car parks, but some only allow parking for a maximum of two hours. Do not leave your car on a meter a moment longer than your time allows and do not return and insert more money once your time has run out – both are finable offences. Most meter parking is free after 6.30pm daily and all day Sunday, but always check on the meter.

Speed Limits: Unless otherwise indicated these are: 30mph (50kph) in urban areas, 60mph (100kph) on normal roads away from built-up areas, 70mph (112kph) on motorways and dual carriageways.

Breakdown: The following organisations operate 24-hour breakdown assistance for members: AA, tel: 0800-887 766, www.theaa.com; RAC, tel: 0800-828 282, www.rac.co.uk.

E

ELECTRICITY

The standard current in Britain is 230-volt, 50-cycle AC. Plugs have three pins, so you need an adaptor.

EMBASSIES

Australia: Australia House, Strand, WC2B; tel: 020-7379 4334; www.australia.org.uk.

Canada: Macdonald House, 1 Grosvenor Square, W1; tel: 020-7258 6600; www.dfait-maeci.gc.ca/canada europa.

Ireland: 17 Grosvenor Place, SW1X; tel: 020-7235 2171; www.embassy ofireland.co.uk.

New Zealand: 80 Haymarket, SW1Y; tel: 020-7930 8422; www.nzembassy.com.

US: 24 Grosvenor Square, W1A; tel: 020-7499 9000; www.usembassy.org.uk.

Pink Paper and *QX*. Monthly magazines for sale include *Gay Times*, *Diva* and *Attitude*.

Useful contacts for advice and counselling include London Lesbian and Gay Switchboard (tel: 020-7837 7324) and London Friend (tel: 020-7837 3337; www.londonfriend.org.uk).

Above from far left: Congestion Charge sign; traffic wardens having a field day.

EMERGENCIES

For police, fire brigade or ambulance dial **999** free from any telephone.

ENTRY REQUIREMENTS

You need a valid passport (or any form of official identification if you are an EU citizen). Visas are not needed if you are from the US, a Commonwealth citizen or an EU national (or from most other European or South American countries). Health certificates are not required unless you have arrived from Asia, Africa or South America. If you wish to stay for a protracted period or apply to work, contact the Border and Immigration Agency (www.ind.homeoffice.gov.uk).

G

GAY AND LESBIAN

With Europe's largest gay and lesbian population, London has an abundance of bars, restaurants and clubs to cater for most tastes, with the scene focusing around Soho, Earl's Court and Vauxhall. For listings, consult the free gay weekly magazines *Boyz*, the

H

HEALTH AND MEDICAL CARE

EU citizens can receive free treatment on producing a European Health Insurance Card. Citizens of other countries must pay, except for emergency treatment (always free). Major hospitals include Charing Cross Hospital (Fulham Palace Road, W6, tel: 020-8846 1234) and St Thomas's (Lambeth Palace Road, SE1, tel: 020-7188 7188). Guy's Hospital Dental Department is at St Thomas Street, SE1, tel: 020-7188 0512. For the nearest hospital or doctor, ring NHS Direct, tel: 0845-46 47. If you need medication outside normal business hours, visit Zafash 24-hour Pharmacy (233–5 Old Brompton Road; tel: 020-3489 0555).

I

INTERNET

Free Wi-fi internet access is becoming increasingly common, in coffee bars, hotels, pubs and bookstores. There are also many internet cafés, where you pay for use by the hour.

Blue Plaques
The first blue ceramic plaque was erected in 1867 on the front of 24 Holles Street, W1, by the Royal Society of Arts to commemorate Lord Byron, who was born there. Across London there are now around 800 such plaques, commemorating former famous residents. Each one gives the bald facts about the person concerned. The awarding of a plaque is haphazard – many are put up after descendants propose the suggestion to English Heritage; however, the person being remembered must have been dead for at least 20 years. The range has so far been dominated by politicians and artists.

L

LEFT LUGGAGE

Most of the main railway stations have left-luggage departments where you can leave suitcases on a short-term basis, although all are extremely sensitive to potential terrorist bombs.

LOST PROPERTY

For possessions lost on public transport or in taxis, contact Transport for London's central Lost Property office (tel: 0845-330 9882), or fill in an enquiry form, available from any London Underground station.

M

MEDIA

Newspapers: Daily national papers include the *Daily Telegraph* and *The Times* (both right of centre politically), *The Independent* (in the middle) and *The Guardian* (left of centre). Most have Sunday equivalents. The *Financial Times* is more business and finance oriented. Except for the *Daily Mirror*, the tabloids (*The Sun, Star, Mail and Express*) are right-wing. The free *Evening Standard* (Mon–Fri) is good for cinema and theatre listings.

Listings Magazines: The weekly *Time Out* is the most comprehensive.

Television: The BBC is financed by annual TV licences; ITV, Channel 4 and Five are funded by advertising. There are also scores of digital, cable and satellite channels to choose from.

Radio: BBC stations include Radio 1 (98.8FM, pop), Radio 2 (89.2FM, easy listening), Radio 3 (91.3FM, classical music), Radio 4 (93.5FM, current affairs, plays, discussions, etc), BBC London (94.9FM, music, chat) and BBC World Service (648 kHz, news). Commercial stations include Capital FM (96.8FM, pop), Jazz FM (102.2FM) and Classic FM (100.9FM).

MONEY

Currency: The monetary unit is the pound sterling (£), divided into 100 pence (p). Bank notes: £5, £10, £20, £50. Coins: 1p, 2p, 5p, 10p, 20p, 50p, £1, £2. Some of London's large stores also accept euros.

Banks: Opening hours are 9.30am–4.30pm Monday to Friday, with Saturday morning banking common in shopping areas. Major British banks tend to offer similar exchange rates, so it is only worth looking around if you have large amounts of money to change. Banks charge no commission on sterling traveller's cheques, and if a London bank is affiliated to your own bank, it will not charge for cheques in other currencies either. However, there will be a charge for changing cash into another currency. You will need ID such as a passport in order to change travellerr's cheques.

ATMs: The easiest way to take out money is using an ATM (cashpoint or cash machine) using your bank card. The best rates are usually available this way. Cash machines can be found

---

Literary Views

For some off-beat views of London, try: *Blimey! - From Bohemia to Britpop*, by Matthew Collings. A funny, readable, and copiously illustrated account of the London art world of the last few decades.

Derelict London by Paul Talling. Nostalgic snapshots that focus on the side of London few tourists see.

London Caffs by Edwin Heathcote gives a tongue-in-cheek survey of a British culinary institution.

London's Disused Underground Stations by J.E.Connor is an intriguing account of the 'ghost' station of London's tube network, accompanied by stunning photographs.

inside and outside banks, in supermarkets and some tube stations. ATMs are accessed using a numeric PIN code.

Credit Cards: International credit cards are almost universally accepted in shops, restaurants and hotels. Signs at the entrance or next to the till should confirm which cards are accepted.

Currency Exchange: Some high-street travel agents, such as Thomas Cook, operate bureaux de change at comparable rates. There are also private bureaux de change (some are open 24 hours), where rates are sometimes very low and commissions very high.

P

POSTAL SERVICES

Most post offices open Mon–Fri 9am–5pm, Sat 9am–noon. Stamps are also available from some shops, usually newsagents, and from machines outside some post offices. There is a two-tier service: first class is supposed to reach a UK destination the next day, second class will take at least a day or two longer. London's main post office (24–8 William IV Street) is by Trafalgar Square, behind the church of St Martin-in-the-Fields and is open 8am–8pm, Mon–Sat.

The cost of sending a letter or parcel depends on weight and size.

PUBLIC HOLIDAYS

1 January: New Year's Day
March/April: Good Friday; Easter Monday.

May: May Day (first Monday); Spring Bank Holiday (last Monday).
August: Summer Bank Holiday (last Monday).
25 December: Christmas Day.
26 December: Boxing Day.

PUBLIC TRANSPORT

Underground (tube)

The fastest and easiest way to get around is by tube. Services run from 5.30am to just after midnight. Always retain your ticket after you have passed through the barrier; you will need it to exit. There is a flat rate of £4 for a single tube journey in any single zone. Oyster Cards *(see box, below)* are a wise buy if you plan to travel a lot by tube (tel: 020-7222 1234; www.tfl.gov.uk).

Above from far left: hugs in Soho; shoppers at the flower market on Columbia Road.

Tickets and Fares

Single tickets on London's transport networks are very expensive, so it's best to buy one of several multi-journey passes. London is divided into six fare zones, with zones 1–2 covering all of central London, and are priced acccording to which zone you travel in. Travelcards give unlimited travel on the tube, buses and DLR. A one-day travelcard for zones 1 and 2, off-peak (valid after 9.30am) costs £6.60. You can also buy three-day or seven-day cards. Oyster cards are smart cards that you charge up with credit (using cash or a credit card), then touch in on card readers at tube stations and on buses, so that an amount is deducted each time you use it. They are cheaper than travelcards if you only expect to travel a few times each day. Cards and Oysters can be bought from tube and DLR stations and from newsagents. Visitors can order them in advance from www.visitbritaindirect.com. For full details of all fares, see www.tfl.gov.uk.

Tube Marathon
There are 275 stations on the Underground network, and the fastest time taken to visit every one currently stands at 19 hours.

Docklands Light Railway
The DLR runs from Bank and Tower Gateway to east and southeast London destinations. Tickets are the same type and cost as for the tube.

Rail
London's commuter rail network provides links to areas not on underground lines; travelcards are valid on rail services for journeys within the correct zones. Thameslink services run through the city centre, while the London Overground connects Richmond with Stratford via the north of the capital. Other services run out of London's major rail stations, including Waterloo, King's Cross, London Bridge, Victoria and Liverpool Street. For times and fares tel: 08457-484 950; www.nationalrail.co.uk.

Bus
If you are not in a hurry, travelling by bus is a good way of seeing London; the bus network is very comprehensive. The flat fare is £2.20. Again, an Oyster Card is the best bet, as each journey then costs £1.30, and the total is price-capped at £4 per day. You can get a seven-day pass for £17.80. Night buses run all night on the most popular routes. Bus route maps are available at Travel Information Centres.

Boat
Thames cruises are a great way to see the sights. Various routes run between Hampton Court and Barrier Gardens. There is a hop-on-hop-off River Rover pass (£13.50; www.citycruises.com).

S

SMOKING

Since July 2007 smoking in all enclosed public spaces, including pubs, clubs and bars (though not in outside beer gardens) has been banned.

STUDENT TRAVELLERS

International students can obtain various discounts at attractions, on travel services (including Eurostar) and in some shops, by showing a valid ISIC card; see www.isiccard.com for details.

T

TAXIS

Black cabs are licensed and display the charges on the meter. They can be hailed in the street if their 'for hire' sign is lit. There are also ranks at major train stations and at various points across the city, or you can order a cab on 0871-871 8710. All black cabs are wheelchair accessible.

Minicabs should only be hired by phone; they are not allowed to pick up passengers on the street. Reputable firms include: Addison Lee, tel: 020-7387 8888; www.addisonlee.com.

TELEPHONES

London's UK dialling code is 020. To call from abroad, dial '44', the international access code for Britain, then 20 (the London code, with the initial

'0' dropped), then the eight-digit individual number.

To phone abroad, dial 00 followed by the international code for the country you want, then the number: Australia (61); Ireland (353); US and Canada (1), etc.

Despite the ubiquity of mobiles (cellphones), London still has a fair number of public phone boxes; most accept phonecards, which are widely available from post offices and newsagents in amounts from £1 to £20. At coin-operated phone boxes, the smallest coin accepted is 20p.

Useful Numbers

Emergency – police, fire, ambulance: tel: 999

Operator (for difficulties in getting through): tel: 100

International Operator: tel: 155

Directory Enquiries (UK): tel: 118 500 or 118 888 or 118 811

International Directory Enquiries: tel: 118 505 or 118 866 or 118 899

TIME

In winter, Great Britain is on Greenwich Mean Time, 8 hours ahead of Los Angeles, 5 hours ahead of New York and Montreal, and 10 hours behind Sydney. From the last Sunday in March to the last Sunday in October, clocks are put forward one hour.

TOUR OPERATORS

The **Original Tour** (tel: 020-8877 2120; www.theoriginaltour.com) runs hop-on-hop-off bus routes in Central London with more than 90 different stops with commentaries available in a variety of languages. There is also a Kids' Club for 5- to 12-year-olds. Purchase tickets on the bus or in advance.

Duck Tours (tel: 020-7928 3132; www.londonducktours.co.uk) employ World War II amphibious vehicles, which leave from County Hall, then drive past famous London landmarks before taking to the water on the Thames. Good fun for children.

TOURIST OFFICES

The official tourist board has its main branch at the Britain and London Visitor Centre, 1 Regent Street, Piccadilly Circus (tel: 08701-566 366; www.visitlondon.com; daily 9.30am–6.30pm).

W

WEBSITES

In addition to the many websites listed in this book, the following are useful: www.bbc.co.uk/london (BBC London) www.thisislondon.com (*Evening Standard* site; useful listings) www.streetmap.co.uk (address locator) www.culture24.org.uk (up-to-date information on museum shows)

WEIGHTS AND MEASURES

Although distances are still measured in miles, and drinks are served as pints, all goods must officially be sold in metric measurements.

Above from far left: buses always come in multiples; black cabs are perfect for foot-weary sightseers.

Tax Refunds for Tourists
Value-Added Tax (VAT), currently 20 percent, is levied on most goods for sale in Britain. Non-EU visitors may claim this back, when spending over a certain amount. A VAT-refund form, available from retailers, needs to be completed and shown to customs on departure, along with all relevant goods and receipts. Ask in shops or at the airport for full details or visit www.hmrc.gov.uk.

Accommodation in London is expensive, but there are some hotels that are destinations in themselves, and some that give a true flavour of the city or the area. There are some excellent deals to be had, too, and a limited amount of good-value budget accommodation.

Covent Garden and Soho

Covent Garden Hotel

10 Monmouth Street, WC2; tel: 020-7806 1000; www.firmdale.com; tube: Covent Garden; £££

Understatedly chic boutique hotel. As well as 58 rooms styled with a contemporary English aesthetic, the hotel also offers a luxurious film screening room, a DVD library, a gym and beauty salon.

Hazlitt's

6 Frith Street, W1; tel: 020-7434 1771; www.hazlittshotel.com; tube: Tottenham Court Road; ££

In the heart of Soho, this gorgeous converted 1718 house has impressive literary connections. Rooms are in period style, and modern luxuries subtly tucked away.

One Aldwych

1 Aldwych, WC2; tel: 020-7300 1000; www.onealdwych.co.uk; tube: Temple, Covent Garden; ££££

Trying a little too hard, with corporate artworks and a pool with underwater music, this hotel nevertheless offers good service in a great location.

St Martin's Lane

45 St Martin's Lane, WC2; tel: 020-7300 5500; www.stmartinslane.com;
tube: Leicester Square; ££££

This Starck/Schrager collaboration is one of the most stylish hotels in town. Rooms have high windows and mood-lighting options. Well placed for West End theatres.

Sanderson Hotel

50 Berners Street, W1; tel: 020-7300 9500; www.sandersonlondon.com; tube: Oxford Circus; ££££

Another Starck/Schrager creation, and the acme of their modernism-meets-theatre ethos. The Long Bar and Suka restaurant are destinations in themselves, and the spa is fittingly opulent.

The Savoy

Strand, WC2; tel: 020-7836 4343; www.fairmont.com/savoy; tube: Charing Cross; ££££

One of London's great institutions, with a reputation for comfort and personal service, reopened after a dramatic £100-million revamp. Conveniently situated for theatreland and Covent Garden.

Soho Hotel

4 Richmond Mews, W1; tel: 020-7559 3000; www.firmdale.com; tube: Tottenham Court Road; £££

With bold, modern design touches in Kit Kemp's signature style, this hotel feels luxuriously urban, with dramatic drawing rooms and a buzzing bar.

W Hotel

Leicester Square, 10 Wardour Street, W1; tel: 020-7758 1000; www.starwoodhotels.com; tube: Piccadilly; ££££

The extraordinary design of the building and its prominent position have already made this new hotel a London landmark. The ultra-sleek nightclub feel of the interior has also made it a fashionable place to be seen.

Brown's Hotel

30 Albemarle Street, W1; tel: 020-7493 6020; www.brownshotel.com; tube: Green Park; ££££

Opened in 1837 by Lord Byron's butler, James Brown, this classic luxury hotel is now owned by Rocco Forte. The interior has been redesigned with a contemporary, elegant look.

Claridge's

Brook Street, W1, tel: 020-7629 8860; www.savoygroup.com; tube: Bond Street; ££££

For many, the embodiment of English hotel graciousness. The rooms are elegant late Victorian or Art Deco in style, and top chef Gordon Ramsay runs the restaurant.

Cumberland Hotel

Great Cumberland Place, W1; tel: 0870 400 8701; www.guoman.com; tube: Marble Arch; ££

Sleek minimalist decor both in the public rooms and the hi-tech guest rooms. Celebrity chef Gary Rhodes runs the restaurant. Good business facilities.

The Dorchester

Park Lane, W1; tel: 020-7629 8888; www.dorchesterhotel.com; tube: Hyde Park Corner; ££££

Large luxury hotel. The rooms have traditional decor and some have views over Hyde Park. The spa and the prestige restaurants – including China Tang and the three-Michelin-starred Alain Ducasse – are the main draw for many.

Duke's Hotel

35 St James's Place, SW1; tel: 020-7491 4840; www.dukeshotel.com; tube: Green Park; £££

Traditional hotel with gas-lamps lighting the courtyard, and an intimate atmosphere. The comfortable rooms are decorated in a classic, understated style. Quality without ostentation.

Durrants Hotel

George Street, W1; tel: 020-7935 8131; www.durrantshotel.co.uk; tube: Marble Arch; ££

A traditional family-run hotel in a Georgian terrace. Rooms are comfortable, with some antique furnishings.

Metropolitan

19 Old Park Lane, W1; tel: 020-7447 1000; www.metropolitan.co.uk; tube: Green Park; ££££

Synonymous with late-1990s celebrity hedonism, the bar is the most noted feature of this modern hotel. The rooms,

Price for a double room for one night without breakfast:	
££££	over £300
£££	£200–300
££	£120–200
£	below £120

Above from far left: the Kipling Suite *(far left)* and swish hotel chair at Brown's Hotel; Soho Hotel; lobby at Duke's Hotel.

Airport Cabins

If you need to bed down at the airport prior to an early morning flight, consider Yotel (tel: 020-7100 1100; www.yotel.com) at Heathrow's Terminal 4 or Gatwick's South Terminal. Here, check into a luxurious cabin (as if in first class on an aircraft) for a few hours' kip at any time of day or night. Depending on demand, a double cabin costs about £80 a night, and a single about £50. Prices come down if you stay for less time (minimum 4 hours, from £30). Cabins have en suite bathrooms, a TV-film system and free internet access.

however, are also worthy of mention, graced as they are with clean simple decor and abundant natural light.

Montcalm Hotel

34–40 Great Cumberland Place, W1; tel: 020-7402 4288; www.montcalm. co.uk; tube: Marble Arch; ££

Quiet, comfortable mid-range hotel in an elegant Georgian crescent. Features low-allergen bedrooms.

No. 5 Maddox Street

5 Maddox Street, W1; tel: 020-7647 0200; www.living-rooms.co.uk; tube: Bond Street; £££

Suites-cum-flats with minimalist, Eastern-inspired decor and full facilities including well-stocked kitchens.

Park Plaza Sherlock Holmes

108 Baker Street, W1; tel: 020-7486 6161; www.parkplazasherlockholmes. com; tube: Baker Street; ££

Ignore the connotations of the name: this is a boutique hotel with modern guest rooms, a gym and a steam room.

Pavilion

34–6 Sussex Gardens, W2; tel: 020-7262 0905; www.pavilionhoteluk. com; tube: Edgware Road; £

Eccentric hotel where each room has a

different theme, from 'Casablanca Nights' to 'Enter the Dragon'.

Piccadilly Backpackers

12 Sherwood Street, W1; tel: 020-7434 9009; www.piccadillyback packers.com; tube: Piccadilly Circus; £

If you are on a tight budget, and more interested in dancing than sleeping, this Soho hostel is ideal. Dorm beds start at £12, and there are also 'pod'-style beds and private rooms.

The Ritz

150 Piccadilly, W1; tel: 020-7493 8181; www.theritzlondon.com; tube: Green Park; ££££

The gilded lustre has long since faded, and this now slightly shabby hotel relies on its famous name to draw people in for highly priced afternoon teas. Men must wear jackets and ties in public rooms; no jeans or trainers allowed.

Westminster and Victoria

B&B Belgravia

64–6 Ebury Street, SW1; tel: 020-7823 4928; www.bb-belgravia.com; tube: Victoria; £

Chic, modern B&B offering good value for the style and facilities. These include: free DVD and internet use, a choice of organic breakfasts, and free bicycle hire.

Eccleston Square Hotel

37 Eccleston Square, SW1; tel: 020-3489 1000; www.ecclestonsquare hotel.com; tube: Victoria; ££

Behind the facade of a smart stuccoed 19th-century town house is probably

---

Price for a double room for one night without breakfast:

££££	over £300
£££	£200–300
££	£120–200
£	below £120

the most technologically sophisticated hotel in London. Each room has a huge 3-D television and DVD player, an iPad2, and electronic settings for everything from the bed and the curtains to lighting and temperature.

Goring Hotel

15 Beeston Place, Grosvenor Gardens, SW1; tel: 020-7396 9000; www.goring hotel.co.uk; tube: Victoria; ££££

This family-owned, delightfully traditional hotel near Buckingham Palace has a relaxed old-world atmosphere.

Sanctuary House Hotel

33 Tothill Street, SW1; tel: 020-7799 4044; www.fullershotels.co.uk; tube: St James's Park; ££

Small, recently refurbished hotel above a Fullers Ale and Pie House.

Kensington and Chelsea

Base2Stay

25 Courtfield Gardens, SW5; tel: 0845-262 8000; www.base2stay. com; tube: Earl's Court; £

Taking the principles and style of boutique hotels to the budget market, this hotel offers 'studios', with their own fridges, microwaves and media facilities.

Beaufort Hotel

33 Beaufort Gardens, SW3; tel: 020-7584 5252; www.thebeaufort.co.uk; tube: Knightsbridge; £££

Soft, neutral colours are indicative of the calm that prevails at this small, designer hotel. Attentive service. Cream teas and residents' bar included in the room rate.

Berkeley Hotel

Wilton Place, SW1; tel: 020-7235 6000; www.the-berkeley.co.uk; tube: Knightsbridge; ££££

Many rate the Berkeley as the best in London. Elegantly low-key, it offers a country-house atmosphere, a fine spa and rooftop pool, and restaurants run by Marcus Wareing and Gordon Ramsay.

Blakes Hotel

33 Roland Gardens, SW7; tel: 020-7370 6701; www.blakeshotel.com; tube: South Kensington; ££££

Anouska Hempel's original design hotel. The discreet exterior belies the splendid rooms, designed variously in romantic, grand and exotic styles.

Cadogan Hotel

75 Sloane Street, SW1; tel: 020-7235 7141; www.cadogan.com; tube: Sloane Square; ££££

An Edwardian-styled hotel with a whiff of scandal permeating its traditional formality. Edward VII's mistress Lillie Langtry lived at the Cadogan, and Oscar Wilde was arrested here.

Capital Hotel

22 Basil Street, SW3; tel: 020-7589 5171; www.capitalhotel.co.uk; tube: Knightsbridge; ££££

This small luxury hotel in the heart of Knightsbridge offers restrained decor, friendly service and a fine restaurant.

easyHotel

14 Lexham Gardens, W8; tel: 07951-440 134; www.easyhotel.com; tube: Gloucester Road; £

Above from far left: The Halkin; guest room (centre left) and decor to impress (centre right) at the Cadogan; Blakes.

Fashionistas' Tea Party
The Berkeley Hotel offers a 'Prêt-à-Portea' afternoon tea with champagne, cakes and pastries inspired by the season's catwalk designs, as well as, if you are interested, tea.

While this is certainly a no-frills experience (some rooms don't even have a window), it is ideal for budget travellers, and has other branches in London. Internet bookings only.

The Gore

189 Queen's Gate, SW7; tel: 020-7584 6601; www.gorehotel.co.uk; tube: South Kensington; £££
Idiosyncratic hotel close to the Royal Albert Hall. Every inch of the walls is covered in paintings and prints, and the themed rooms are decorated with antiques and many a theatrical flourish.

Halkin Hotel

5–6 Halkin Street, SW1; tel: 020-7333 1000; www.halkin.como.bz; tube: Hyde Park Corner; ££££
This modern five-star hotel, done out in a minimalist Italian aesthetic, is calm and cosseting, if a little impersonal. Houses London's only Michelin-starred Thai restaurant.

The Rockwell

181 Cromwell Road, SW5; tel: 020-7244 2000; www.therockwellhotel.com; tube: Earl's Court; ££
Decorated in a contemporary homely style, the rooms feel cheerful and airy.

Price for a double room for one night without breakfast:	
££££	over £300
£££	£200–300
££	£120–200
£	below £120

Vicarage Private Hotel

10 Vicarage Gate, W8; tel: 020-7229 4030; www.londonvicaragehotel.com; tube: Notting Hill Gate; £
Friendly place, with clean, simple rooms and good English breakfasts.

Bloomsbury and Holborn

Academy Hotel

21 Gower Street, WC1; tel: 020-7631 4115; www.theetoncollection.com; tube: Goodge Street; ££
A welcoming boutique hotel, situated in five interlinked town houses. Comfortable rooms with traditional decor.

Charlotte Street Hotel

15–17 Charlotte Street, W1; tel: 020-7806 2000; www.firmdale.com; tube: Goodge Street; £££
Combines old-fashioned quality and contemporary style, with soft colours and bold touches. There is a luxurious cinema in the basement.

Crescent Hotel

49–50 Cartwright Gardens, WC1; tel: 020-7387 1515; www.crescent hoteloflondon.com; tube: Russell Square, Euston; £
Simple but pleasant family-run hotel in a Georgian building. Also has access to private gardens and tennis courts.

Hotel Russell

Russell Square, WC1; tel: 020-7837 6470; www.principal-hayley.com; tube: Russell Square; ££
A Bloomsbury landmark with opulent public spaces and individually styled bedrooms in calm understated colours.

The City and East London

ANdAZ

40 Liverpool Street, EC2; tel: 020-7961 1234; www.london.liverpool street.andaz.com; tube: Liverpool Street; £££

ANdAZ fits designer facilities into a Victorian railway hotel. Rooms are simple and contemporary in style.

Fox & Anchor

115 Charterhouse Street, Smithfield, EC1; tel: 020-7250 1300; www.fox andanchor.com; tube: Barbican; £–££

This immaculately restored pub has six individually styled rooms combining modern comforts with period features.

The Hoxton Urban Lodge

81 Great Eastern Street, Old Street, EC2; tel: 020-7550 1000; www. hoxtonhotels.com; tube: Old Street; £

The well-designed rooms offer outstanding value and the latest in hipster chic. Watch the website for the periodic offers of rooms for only £1.

Malmaison

Charterhouse Square, Clerkenwell, EC1; tel: 020-7012 3700; www. malmaison.com; tube: Barbican; £££

Atmosphere and style without sky-high rates in a beautiful Victorian building. Rooms are designed with stylish fabrics and smart bathrooms; the brasserie and bar come highly recommended.

The Rookery

12 Peter's Lane, Cowcross Street; tel: 020-7336 0931; www.rookery hotel.com; tube: Farringdon; £££

Has wood panelling, stone-flagged floors, and open fires. Spacious rooms combine the historic with the contemporary: 18th-century beds and flat-screen TVs.

Threadneedles

5 Threadneedle Street, EC2; tel: 020-7657 8080; www.theeton collection.com; tube: Bank; £££

Located in a former bank building, this five-star hotel blends modern comforts with Victorian splendour.

Zetter Restaurant & Rooms

86–8 Clerkenwell Road, EC1; tel: 020-7324 4444; www.thezetter.com; tube: Farringdon; ££

A quirky designer hotel in a converted warehouse. Second-hand books and hot-water bottles are thoughtful extras in the chic, comfortable rooms. Also check www.thezettertownhouse.com in nearby St John Square.

South Bank and Bankside

Mad Hatter

3–7 Stamford Street, SE1; tel: 020-7401 9222; www.fullershotels.co.uk; tube: London Bridge, Southwark; ££

Large, colourful, contemporary-styled rooms above a Fullers pub, just a short stroll from Tate Modern.

Southwark Rose

47 Southwark Bridge Road, SE1; tel: 020-7015 1480; www.all-seasons-hotels.com; tube: London Bridge; ££

Sleek, simply designed hotel with clean, minimalist lines. Friendly staff.

Above from far left: grand exterior *(far left)* and guest room *(centre left)* at ANdAZ, formerly the Great Eastern Hotel; guest room *(centre right)* and funky staircase at Zetter Restaurant & Rooms.

Facts and Figures According to Visit London, the capital's tourist board, there are more than 100,000 rooms in the city as a whole, providing accommodation for over 27 million overnight visitors each year. This makes it the world's most popular city destination.

Food from all over the world as well as good British staples, and chefs with innovative ways of preparing fresh home-grown ingredients, can be found in a wide range of prices and environments throughout the capital.

Covent Garden and Soho

Andrew Edmunds

46 Lexington Street, W1; tel: 020-7437 5708; daily L and D; tube: Piccadilly Circus; £££

Soft candlelight and wood panelling make this place cosy and intimate. Dishes are simple but varied, ranging from beef to well-presented pasta. The staff are relaxed and friendly.

Café Emm

17 Frith Street, W1; tel: 020-7437 0723; www.cafeemm.com; daily L and D; tube: Leicester Square; £–££

Convivial and exceptionally good value, and packed every night. Large portions of fish cakes, lamb shanks and fish and chips. Beware of queues and occasional boisterous birthday parties.

The Ivy

1 West Street, WC2; tel: 020-7836 4751; www.the-ivy.co.uk; daily L and D; tube: Covent Garden; £££–££££

Price guide for an average two-course meal for one with a glass of house wine:

££££	over £40
£££	£25–£40
££	£15–25
£	below £15

A place to see and be seen, and the food is a secondary consideration, though of decent quality (British classics plus international favourites). The downside is the difficulty in getting a table: reserve weeks, not days, ahead.

Koya

49 Frith Street, W1; tel: 020-7434 4463; www.koya.co.uk; Mon–Sat L and D; tube: Leicester Square; ££

There's always a queue outside, and they don't take reservations. The udon noodles, and pork belly, at this minimalist Japanese canteen are stupendous.

Mildreds

45 Lexington Street, W1; tel: 020-7494 1634; www.mildreds.co.uk; Mon–Sat L and D; tube: Piccadilly Circus; £

Sleek and stylish vegetarian restaurant which offers porcini and ale pie and Malaysian coconut curry.

Mr Kong

21 Lisle Street, WC2; tel: 020-7437 7341; www.mrkongrestaurant.com; daily L and D; tube: Leicester Square; £–££

One of the more authentic Chinese restaurants in the area. Dishes include Kon Chi baby squid with chilli sauce or sandstorm crab. Vegetarian options.

Polpetto

49 Dean Street, W1; tel: 020-7437 2477; www.polpetto.co.uk; Mon–Sat L and D; tube: Leicester Square; £££

In a room above the French House pub, Polpetto offers good food, well-priced

wine and excellent service. The zucchini fries and breaded sardines are delicious.

Rules

35 Maiden Lane, WC2; tel: 020-7836 5314; www.rules.co.uk; daily L and D; tube: Covent Garden; £££

Established in 1798, the decor reflects its heritage and the food has stood the test of time with high-quality British ingredients: beef, lamb and game from Rules' own estate. Booking advisable.

J Sheekey

28–32 St Martin's Court, WC2; tel: 020-7240 2565; www.j-sheekey.co.uk; daily L and D; tube: Leicester Square; £££–££££

A paradise for fish lovers, in a series of panelled rooms hung with black-and-white theatre prints: specialities include char-grilled squid with gorgonzola polenta, Cornish fish stew and New England baby lobster. Pre-theatre dinners a speciality. Reserve.

Stockpot

18 Old Compton Street, W1; tel: 020-7287 1066; www.stockpotlondon.co.uk; daily L and D; tube: Leicester Square; £

'The Pot' has been going for years, serving basic food at very low prices. Also on King's Road and Panton Street.

Mayfair and Piccadilly

Benares

12a Berkeley Square House, Berkeley Square, W1; tel: 020-7629 8886; www.benaresrestaurant.com; daily L and D; tube: Bond Street; £££

Atul Kochhar's Benares is one of the few Indian restaurants in Europe to win a Michelin star. Dishes include Goan-style lobster Masala in coconut and cinnamon sauce. Reservations essential.

Criterion Grill

224 Piccadilly, W1; tel: 020-7930 0488; www.criterionrestaurant.com; Mon–Sat L and D; tube: Piccadilly Circus; ££–£££

This beautifully restored Victorian restaurant has a simple menu of French classics, all decently prepared. The opulent neo-Byzantine interior is wonderful, and the pre-theatre set menu is reasonably priced.

Greens Restaurant and Oyster Bar

36 Duke Street, SW1; tel: 020-7930 4566; www.greens.org.uk; daily L and D; tube: Green Park; £££

Clubby St James's stalwart. Traditional dishes include potted shrimps and lemon sole with perfect hollandaise. Excellent cheeseboard.

Guinea Grill

30 Bruton Place, W1; tel: 020-7499 1210; www.theguinea.co.uk; Mon–Fri L and D, Sat D; tube: Oxford Circus, Green Park; £££

Old-world, wood-panelled place in a cobbled mews. Great steak and kidney pie, grills and oysters. Good choice of beers, wines and ports.

Scotts

20 Mount Street, W1; tel: 020-7629 5248; www.scotts-restaurant.com;

Above from far left: organic duck with lentils; the stylish RIBA café (see p.49); tempting cocktail; fish and chips with mushy peas.

Eating Out with Children
This need not be an ordeal. Although the maître d's face in many a smart restaurant may fall as you approach with a gaggle of tots in tow, there are some establishments that enjoy catering for children. Try Sticky Fingers (Phillimore Gardens, W8 7QG; www.stickyfingers.co.uk), the children's restaurants in Harrods and Hamley's, or any of the cafés in London's parks. Look out also for branches of Giraffe (South Bank, Spitalfields Market, Brunswick Centre etc), Pizza Express and Carluccio's (all over London), which are usually very child-friendly.

daily L and D; tube: Marble Arch, Green Park; £££

This revamped institution continues to serve delicious fish dishes, including rarities such as stargazy pie. The old-fashioned puddings get a modern twist.

Sketch

9 Conduit Street, W1; tel: 0870 777 44 88; www.sketch.uk.com; Lecture Room Mon–Sat L and D, Gallery Mon–Sat D only; tube: Bond Street, Oxford Circus; ££££

It's decadently over-designed, and super-chef Pierre Gagnaire's food is dizzily priced. Choose between the haute cuisine Lecture Room and the more informal Gallery, where, apparently, 'art meets food meets fashion'.

Westminster and Victoria

Bistrot on the Square

37 Eccleston Square, SW1; tel: 020-3489 1000; www.ecclestonsquare hotel.com; daily B, Br, L, AT and D; tube: Victoria; ££

Stylish restaurant in the new Eccleston Square Hotel serves old favourites from kedgeree to steak and chips, and club sandwiches to schnitzels, all executed with care and panache.

Price guide for an average two-course meal for one with a glass of house wine:	
££££	over £40
£££	£25–£40
££	£15–25
£	below £15

La Poule au Pot

231 Ebury Street SW1; tel: 020-7730 7763; www.pouleaupot.co.uk; daily L and D; tube: Sloane Square; ££–£££

This romantic spot has been here for 30 years. Everything is very fresh and very French. Good-value set lunches.

Kensington and Chelsea

Bibendum

Michelin House, 81 Fulham Road, SW3; tel: 020-7581 5817; www. bibendum.co.uk; daily L and D; tube: South Kensington; £££

Located in the Art Deco Michelin building. Chef Matthew Harris maintains high standards. Grilled oysters with curried sauce and courgette linguine are faultless, the wine list is good and service excellent. Good-value fixed-price lunch menus. Reserve.

Cambio de Tercio

163 Old Brompton Road, SW5; tel: 020-7244 8970; www.cambiode tercio.co.uk; daily L and D; tube: Gloucester Road; ££–£££

This bright, cheery little restaurant has won many accolades for its exciting food and impeccable service. Some think it is the best Spanish restaurant in town.

Chutney Mary

535 King's Road, SW10; tel: 020-7351 3113; www.chutneymary.com; Mon–Fri D only, Sat–Sun L and D; tube: Fulham Broadway; £££

First-class Indian restaurant with stylish decor and exceptional food. The chefs come from across the subcontinent, so take your pick of regional dishes.

Restaurant Gordon Ramsay

68–9 Royal Hospital Road, SW3; tel: 020-7352 4441/3334; www.gordon ramsay.com; Mon–Fri L and D; tube: Sloane Square; ££££

The decor is minimalist, the experience impeccable. One of only four restaurants in Britain with three Michelin stars. Try chargrilled monkfish tail with crispy duck. Prices are high so consider the excellent set lunch menu.

Tom Aikens

43 Elystan Street, SW3; tel: 020-7584 2003; www.tomaikens.co.uk; Tue–Fri L and D, Sat D only; tube: South Kensington; ££££

Michelin-starred modern French restaurant. Intensely flavoured dishes such as pig's head braised with spices and ginger demonstrate Aikens' culinary craftsmanship and flair.

Bloomsbury and Holborn

Fryer's Delight

19 Theobald's Road, WC1; tel: 020-7405 4114; Mon–Sat noon–10pm; tube: Holborn; £

One of the few remaining fish and chip shops in central London.

Leith's

113 Chancery Lane, WC2; tel: 020-7316 5580; www.leiths.com; Mon–Fri L (snack menu 5–9pm); tube: Chancery Lane; ££

An offshoot of Leith's Cookery School, this relaxed place is ideal for a light, fresh lunch. The menu may include citrus-crusted lamb rump or spinach and blue cheese gnocchi.

Pied à Terre

34 Charlotte Street, W1; tel: 020-7636 1178; www.pied-a-terre.co.uk; Mon–Fri L and D, Sat D only; tube: Goodge Street; ££££

Fitzrovia's most prestigious restaurant under chef Marcus Eaves has two Michelin stars. The eight-course tasting menu is £80, but set lunch is a bargain.

The City

Bistro du Vin,

40 St John Street, Clerkenwell, EC1; tel: 020-7490 9230; www.bistroduvin andbar.com; daily L and D, Sat–Sun Br; tube: Barbican; ££

In a fine Victorian building near Smithfield Market, this bistro has comfortable seating and a relaxed atmosphere. Tuck into roast leg of lamb with potatoes dauphinoise and try one of the 200 wines (many available by the glass).

Clark's

46 Exmouth Market, EC1; tel: 020-7837 1974; Mon–Sat, all day; tube: Farringdon; £

One of London's few remaining pie and mash shops, with worn wooden pews, tiled floors, low prices and no-nonsense service. Cash only.

Coach & Horses

26–8 Ray Street, EC1; tel: 020-7657 8088; www.thecoachandhorses.com; Mon–Fri L and D, Sat D only, Sun L only; tube: Farringdon; ££

One of the best of the gastro-pubs. The scrubbed-wood decor is simple, the food inventive but unpretentious, the wines well priced and the service good.

Above from far left: Sketch; invitation to the bar; home-made ice cream at the Seven Stars *(see p.56)*; petals at the Cinammon Club *(see p.29)*.

Tipping
In Britain it is customary to add 10 percent to the bill for service. Be careful, though, that you do not pay for service twice, since many restaurants add this (or more often 12 percent) to the bill automatically. Of course, if you are less than satisfied with the service, do not hesitate to leave a smaller tip, or none at all. You might also check with the waiting staff whether they get to keep the tips or whether the management pockets them instead.

The Eagle

159 Farringdon Road, EC1; tel: 020-7837 1353; Mon–Sat L and D, Sun L only; tube: Farringdon; ££

Pub serving reasonable food with a Mediterranean bias, complemented by an extensive range of European beers. Gets crowded quickly, so arrive early.

Fox & Anchor

115 Charterhouse Street, Smithfield, EC1; tel: 020-7250 1300; www.foxandanchor.com; daily B, L and D; tube: Barbican; ££

Old-fashioned British cooking in a lovingly restored pub. Try the oysters with a pint of stout (in a pewter tankard), followed by ham hock, steak and oyster pie or the daily roast. Prices are very reasonable and the atmosphere relaxed. Highly recommended.

Moro

34–6 Exmouth Market, EC1; tel: 020-7833 8336; www.moro.co.uk; Mon–Fri L and D, Sat D only; tube: Farringdon; ££

The excellent food on Moro's lively Spanish–North African menu includes charcoal grilled lamb and wood-roasted pork. Friendly service.

St John

26 St John Street, EC1; tel: 020-7251 0848; www.stjohnrestaurant.com; Mon–Fri L and D, Sat D only, Sun L only; tube: Farringdon; £££

A stone's throw from Smithfield meat market, this restaurant is stark but elegant. The meat- and offal-heavy menu changes with the season. Chef Fergus Henderson's signature roast bone-marrow and parsley salad is always on the menu, and whole roast suckling pig may make an appearance.

Smiths of Smithfield

66–7 Charterhouse Street, EC1; tel: 020-7251 7950; www.smithsofsmithfield.co.uk; daily B, L and D; tube: Farringdon; ££–£££ (brunch Sat–Sun ££)

Brunch on a Saturday or Sunday is great fun in this buzzing post-industrial complex. Tuck into a cooked breakfast, grilled minute steak, or corned beef hash. The restaurant upstairs is more refined and more expensive.

The South Bank

The Anchor and Hope

36 The Cut, SE1; tel: 020-7928 9898; Tue–Sat L and D, Sun L only, Mon D only; tube: Waterloo; ££

All the produce here is British, and the meat – featured strongly on the menu – is butchered on the premises. Try the perfectly cooked roast neck of lamb with ratatouille. Keen prices, hefty portions and friendly staff. No reservations.

The Fish Place

Battersea, SW11; tel: 020-7095 0410; www.thefishplace.co.uk; Tue–Sat L and D, Sun L only; tube: Clapham Junction; £££

One of London's best fish and seafood restaurants just beside London Heliport with panoramic views over the river. The freshest fish is cooked with judgement and flair. Signature dishes include sautéed River Dart mussels,

Dorset crab ravioli and steamed fillet of wild sea bass. The set-price two-course lunch is an absolute bargain.

Masters Super Fish

191 Waterloo Road, SE1; tel: 020-7928 6924; Tue–Sat L and D, Mon D only; tube: Waterloo; £

Need a taxi? You will find cabbies galore tucking into huge portions of fish and chips in this old-fashioned eatery.

Mesón Don Felipe

53 The Cut, SE1; tel: 020-7928 3237; www.mesondonfelipe.com; Mon–Sat L and D, Sun D; tube: Southwark; ££

A busy little place with a great atmosphere and lots of tasty tapas. The drinks list is an education in Spanish wines. Bookings taken before 8pm; after that it is first come first served.

East London

Fifteen

15 Westland Place, N1; tel: 0871-330 1515; www.fifteen.net; daily B, L and D; tube: Old Street; £££

Run by Jamie Oliver, every year this restaurant apprentices disadvantaged young people into its kitchen and tries to transform them into Italian chefs that even The River Café would be

---

Price guide for an average two-course meal for one with a glass of house wine:

££££	over £40
£££	£25–£40
££	£15–25
£	below £15

---

proud of. Even if the dishes are not always perfectly executed, it is fascinating to see this project in action.

The Real Greek & Mezedopolio

14–15 Hoxton Market, N1; tel: 020-7739 8212; www.therealgreek.com; daily L and D; tube: Old Street; ££

Mezze regulars are moussakas, tiny shellfish and tomato cutlets. Main courses include lamb or beef pasta dishes, and there are distinctive cheeses and pastries.

Story Deli

3 Dray Walk, The Old Truman Brewery, 91 Brick Lane, E1; tel: 020-7247 3137; daily B, L and D; tube: Liverpool Street; £

This organic pizzeria is easily missed from the street, but worth seeking out, not only for its outstanding pizzas, but also for tasty kebabs, sandwiches, scrumptious cakes and coffee.

West London

The River Café

Thames Wharf, Rainville Road, W6; tel: 020-7386 4200; www.rivercafe.co.uk; Mon–Sat L and D, Sun L only; tube: Hammersmith; £££–££££

A west London institution, and its reputation for fine Italian food is well deserved (as is its reputation for very high prices). Only the best produce is selected by owner/chef, Ruth Rogers. Dishes such as char-grilled scallops with deep-fried artichokes, beef with tomatoes and spinach are faultless. Booking well ahead is essential.

Above from far left: Regent's Park's Honest Sausage *(see p.49)*; mallards' legs at St John; daily specials on the blackboard; one of the capital's many trendy restaurants.

School Puddings
Many British people retain a particular fondness for the traditional puddings of their schooldays. These include treacle sponge pudding, jam roly poly, trifle, bread-and-butter pudding, sticky toffee pudding, apple Charlotte, rhubarb crumble and rice pudding – many of them considerably enhanced with a good dollop of custard. Children's author Enid Nesbit summed up the peculiar satisfaction of one such pudding as follows: 'Jam roly gives you a peaceful feeling and you do not at first care if you never play any run-about game ever any more.'

These entertainment venues represent a selection of the landmarks of London's vibrant cultural scene. You could also consult www.viewlondon. co.uk or the weekly listings magazine, *Time Out*, which is available from all good newagents.

Theatre

National Theatre
South Bank; tel: 020-7452 3000; www.nationaltheatre.org.uk
One of Britain's most famous modernist buildings contains three theatres, which present a range of modern and classical drama.

The Old Vic
The Cut, near Waterloo Station; tel: 0844-871 7628; www.oldvictheatre.com
This former music hall is now a repertory theatre with a strong reputation. Kevin Spacey is the artistic director.

Royal Court Theatre
Sloane Square; tel: 020-7565 5000; www.royalcourttheatre.com
This stylish venue stages plays by contemporary playwrights. The bar-restaurant in the foyer is ideal for pre-theatre dinners.

Shakespeare's Globe
21 New Globe Walk, Bankside; tel: 020-7902 1500; www.shakespeares-globe.org
A reconstruction of Shakespeare's original open-to-the-elements theatre, the Globe hosts summer seasons of his, and other, plays.

Music

Barbican Arts Centre
Silk Street; tel: 020-7638 8891; www.barbican.org.uk
A purpose-built arts complex with a theatre, cinema, and art gallery as well an impressive concert hall. The venue for the London Symphony Orchestra.

London Coliseum
St Martin's Lane; tel: 0871-911 0200; www.eno.org
This extravagantly decorated Edwardian theatre is home to the English National Opera.

Ronnie Scott's
47 Frith Street; tel: 020-7439 0747; www.ronniescotts.co.uk
The eclectic musical tastes of Ronnie Scott, who died in 1996, are still reflected in this legendary Soho venue, which has hosted some of the biggest names in jazz since 1959.

Royal Albert Hall
Kensington Gore; tel: 020-7589 8212; www.royalalberthall.com
This vast rotunda hosts large-scale concerts by ageing rock stars and occasional operatic performances, as well as the Promenade festival of classical concerts throughout the summer.

Royal Festival Hall
Belvedere Road; tel: 0871-663 2500; www.southbankcentre.co.uk
As well as being the premier classical music venue, this complex offers free Friday lunch time jazz and folk performances in the foyer.

NIGHTLIFE

Royal Opera House

Bow Street, Covent Garden; tel:
020-7304 4000; www.roh.org.uk

Home to the Royal Ballet and the
Royal Opera, this magnificent theatre
has a worldwide reputation.

Above from far
left: Royal Albert
Hall; Alistair
Spalding, Artistic
Director of Sadler's
Wells; The Old Vic
theatre; Café de
Paris.

Dance

Peacock Theatre

Portugal Street; tel: 0844-412 4322;
www.sadlerswells.com

This outpost of Sadler's Wells in the
West End is housed in an uninspiring
concrete block, but visitors shouldn't
be put off – the modern dance productions staged here are usually first rate.

Sadler's Wells

Rosebery Avenue; tel: 0844-412
4300; www.sadlerswells.com

This hi-tech theatre near Islington in
North London is Britain's top contemporary dance venue.

Film

BFI Southbank

Belvedere Road, South Bank; tel:
020-7928 3232; www.bfi.org.uk

The headquarters of the British Film
Institute presents a varied programme
of arthouse and off-beat films on
three screens.

Curzon Soho

99 Shaftesbury Avenue; tel: 020-7292
1686; www.curzoncinemas.com

This is the flagship in a chain of five
arts cinemas in London. The other
branches are in Bloomsbury, Chelsea,
Mayfair and Richmond. Each branch
screens all the latest arthouse releases.

Prince Charles Cinema

7 Leicester Place; tel: 020 7494 3654;
www.princecharlescinema.com

The big multiplexes on nearby
Leicester Square charge high prices for
blockbuster films but this quirky little
cinema round the corner offers a more
interesting repertory programme at a
more modest price.

Bars and Clubs

Café de Paris

3–4 Coventry Street; tel: 020-7734
7700; www.cafedeparis.com

The Café de Paris is a stylish old
dancehall which attracts an older
crowd that likes to dress up smartly.

Cargo

83 Rivington Street; tel: 020-7739
3440; www.cargo-london.com

This gritty under-the-arches venue is
a staple part of big nights out in
Shoreditch. Entertainment includes
live music, DJs and dancing till late.

EGG

5–13 Vale Royal; tel: 020-7609 8364;
www.egglondon.net

A venue with three dance floors, EGG
attracts big-name DJs, and is also
noted for its gay nights.

Electric Ballroom

184 Camden High Street; tel: 020-
7485 9006; www.electricballroom.
co.uk

This old dancehall attracts a mixed
crowd with its retro 1970s, 1980s and
1990s nights. Upstairs there's R&B .
and hip-hop.

CREDITS

Insight Step by Step London
Written and updated by: Michael Macaroon
Commissioning Editor: Catherine Dreghorn
Series Editor: Carine Tracanelli
Picture Editor: Ian Spick
Photography by: Apa: Natasha Babaian, David Beatty, Jay Fechtman, Glyn Genin, Tony Halliday, Britta Jaschinski, Sian Lezard, Michael Macaroon, Clare Peel, Dorothy Stannard, Sarah Sweeney, Ming Tang-Evans except: AKG 44TR; Alamy 12TR, 13TL, 13BR, 22/3, 82TL, 85T; ANdaZ/Hyatt 114TL, 114TR; William Beckett 30C; Brown's Hotel 110TL, 110TR; Cadogan Hotel 112TR, 113TL; Cafe de Paris 123; Julian Calder 53TR; Corbis 37T, 71TL, 81T; Duke's Hotel 111TR; Getty 11CBR; Halkin Hotel 112TL; Courtesy Harrods 19BR; iStock 57T; Old Vic 123TL; Olympic Delivery Authority 11ML, 92T; Pavel Libera 10TL; Alisdair Macdonald 22/3T, 103, 104, 105, 108, 109; James Macdonald 39BR; Rob Moore 26T; Press Association 93T; Courtesy Madame Tussauds 47B; National Portrait Gallery 35TL; ©RBG Kew 6BR, 98TL, 98TR, 99TL, 99TR, 99B; Sadlers Wells 122R; Scala 33T, 34B, 34TL, 76TR, Science & Society Picture Library 79BR; Soho Hotel 111TL; SuperStock 55T; ©Tate 70TL; ©Tate. Photo: Andy Paradise 68TL; ©Tate 2007 70CL; Courtesy of Visit London 10TR, 11TR, 12TL, 26TL, 26TR, 28TL, 32T, 41TR, 41BR, 42TL, 66BL, 69TL, 77TL, 82TR, 87TR, 91TR; Adam Woolfitt/Robert Harding 10BL, 14TL; V&A 77BR; Zetter 115TL, 115TR.
Front Cover: photolibrary.com; 4Corners Images, Ming Tang-Evans/APA. **Back Cover:** Fotolia.

Printed by: CTPS – China

Maps based on OpenStreetMap data ©OpenStreetMap contributors, CC-BY-SA. Produced by Phoenix Mapping Ltd. Updated by APA Cartography Department.

DISTRIBUTION

Worldwide
Apa Publications GmbH & Co. Verlag KG (Singapore branch)
7030 Ang Mo Kio Ave 5,
08-65 Northstar @ AMK, Singapore 569880
Email: apasin@singnet.com.sg

UK and Ireland
Dorling Kindersley Ltd,
a Penguin Group company
80 Strand, London WC2R 0RL, UK

United States
Ingram Publisher Services
One Ingram Blvd, PO Box 3006,
La Vergne, TN 37086-1986
customer.service@ingrampublisherservices.com

Australia
Universal Publishers
PO Box 307, St Leonards, NSW 1590
Email: sales@universalpublishers.com.au

CONTACTING THE EDITORS

We would appreciate it if readers would alert us to errors or outdated information by writing to us at insight@apaguide.co.uk or Apa Publications, PO Box 7910, London SE1 1WE, UK.

www.insightguides.com

INDEX